PRAISE FOR *TAILOR MADE*

Tailor Made is a powerful book and a must-read for every generation. Alex Seeley dares to share her own story of discovering who she really is in a raw and authentic way—writing about how the process of becoming is the actual destination and how to embrace and navigate those seasons to find the freedom to be who God created you to be. I highly recommend this book because more than ever we need to know who God says we are so we can be confident to do what He has predestined us to do.

—Christine Caine,
Founder of A21 and Propel Women

My friend Alex is a force! The inspiring words of *Tailor Made* will help you shed the limiting labels of your past and position you to draw near to our Master Tailor Father. We were made for intimacy, not imitation. In Alex's words, "You are not one-size-fits-all; you are tailor-made by the Designer of the universe." It's time to live this truth!

—Lisa Bevere,
New York Times bestselling
author of *Without Rival*

Alex has an incredibly deep understanding of God's Word, but the way she lives, teaches, and writes is also marked by her vibrant relationship with the Holy Spirit that permeates everything about her. Through her transparency and honesty, we can all recognize pieces of our own brokenness as she shares hers. But through her restoration and wholeness, we also see the healing and transformation that is available. I'm blessed and honored to call Alex my pastor and friend. With truth, humility, and love, she helps readers unlock deep places in their hearts that still need healing—helping many begin to live in the fullness of God's personal design He has tailor-made for every life. I know this book is doing that for me.

—Natalie Grant,
Five-time Female Artist of the Year
for the Gospel Music Association

Alex Seeley's book *Tailor Made* is a right-now message for a culture that has been inundated with so many negative voices through social media, entertainment, and the Internet. Never before has it been so easy to fall into the trap of comparison and allow feelings of inadequacy to unknowingly cause us to fall off track and change us into who we were not fully meant to be. I was deeply moved by the way Alex used her story of heartbreak and pain woven through Gods' glorious plan of redemption to be an example of hope to anyone who reads it. I devoured this book and found myself wanting to read it again because of the impact of her message. Whether you have served the Lord for thirty days or thirty years, I highly recommend this book.

—Danny Gokey,

Grammy-nominated and Dove

Award–winning artist

Alex Seeley is both a dear friend and one of the most effective ministers I've ever met. She consistently mines jewels out of the Holy Scriptures that I've tripped over in the past but never seen or appreciated until she held them up to the glorious light of the gospel. *Tailor Made* will absolutely help you fall more in love with Jesus and lead you further into the abundant, joyful, holy, purposeful, world-changing life He's called us to!

—Lisa Harper,

Bible teacher and bestselling author

Alex is inviting us into the deep rooms of her heart, sharing her life and testimony, which powerfully portray a redemptive story of grace and vulnerability from the first page to the last. One of the biggest challenges of our time is authenticity, and it's refreshing to read a piece of writing from an influential leader who is sharing her journey in such a transparent way.

Alex points us to the truth that the **process** is the destination; that the Great Designer of the Universe is able to create, shape, and tailor-make our brokenness into something beautiful—into more then we could ever dream, ask, or imagine. Read *Tailor Made* and be set free from the fear of man, religion, and shame.

—Jonas Myrin,

Grammy Award–winning

singer and songwriter.

There are few voices as impactful in my life as Alex Seeley. Her words cut to the center of me and remain there, bringing truth and light and joy and peace. This story will remind you of your past, bless your present, and give you power and faith for the future you've always wanted.

—Annie F. Downs,
Bestselling author of *100 Days to Brave* and *Looking for Lovely*

Tailor Made is a refreshing revelation of who our Creator is and why He created us. It feels like an eyewitness account straight out of Heaven. If there was one book I wish the world could read, this would be it. Alex's story points back to the work of the Author and Finisher of our faith, uncovering our purpose and filling in every void like only God can. I am grateful and honored to know Alex Seeley as a friend, pastor, preacher, and now as an author.

—Chris Durso,
Author of *The Heist: How Grace Robs Us of Our Shame*

I have read this book from cover to cover—some chapters multiple times—as I was compelled to ponder, pray, and chew on its content. I have rarely read a manuscript that has so captured my attention, kept me wondering what the next chapter would bring, and made me feel like I really got to know the author in a deep, real-life manner. Alex Seeley has a gift for storytelling. She also has a rare capacity to meet a person right where they are and encourage and challenge them to their next place in God's plan. *Tailor Made* is designed exactly in that way—with the potential to alter the spiritual DNA of an entire generation.

—Dr. James W. Goll,
Founder of God Encounters Ministries,
international author and Life Language trainer

TAILORMADE

TAILORMADE

Discover the Secret to Who God Created You to Be

ALEX SEELEY

W PUBLISHING GROUP

AN IMPRINT OF THOMAS NELSON

Published in Nashville, Tennessee, by W Publishing, an imprint of Thomas Nelson.

Author is represented by the literary agency of Alive Communications, Inc., 7680 Goddard Street, Suite 200, Colorado Springs, CO, 80920.

Thomas Nelson titles may be purchased in bulk for educational, business, fund-raising, or sales promotional use. For information, please e-mail SpecialMarkets@ ThomasNelson.com.

Unless otherwise noted, Scripture quotations are taken from the Holy Bible, New International Version®, NIV®. Copyright © 1973, 1978, 1984, 2011 by Biblica, Inc.® Used by permission of Zondervan. All rights reserved worldwide. www.Zondervan.com. The "NIV" and "New International Version" are trademarks registered in the United States Patent and Trademark Office by Biblica, Inc.®

Scripture quotations marked AMP are from the Amplified® Bible. Copyright © 1954, 1958, 1962, 1964, 1965, 1987 by The Lockman Foundation. Used by permission. (www.Lockman.org)

Scripture quotations marked MSG are from The Message. Copyright © by Eugene H. Peterson 1993, 1994, 1995, 1996, 2000, 2001, 2002. Used by permission of NavPress. All rights reserved. Represented by Tyndale House Publishers, Inc.

Scripture quotations marked NLT are from the Holy Bible, New Living Translation. © 1996, 2004, 2007, 2013, 2015 by Tyndale House Foundation. Used by permission of Tyndale House Publishers, Inc., Carol Stream, Illinois 60188. All rights reserved.

Any Internet addresses, phone numbers, or company or product information printed in this book are offered as a resource and are not intended in any way to be or to imply an endorsement by Thomas Nelson, nor does Thomas Nelson vouch for the existence, content, or services of these sites, phone numbers, companies, or products beyond the life of this book.

ISBN 978-0-7852-1533-2 (eBook)

Library of Congress Control Number: 2017050246

ISBN 978-0-7180-7505-7 (TP)

Printed in the United States of America

18 19 20 21 22 LSC 10 9 8 7 6 5 4 3

To my husband, Henry. Thank you for showing me what true love looks like and for never letting me settle for mediocrity. I could not have done this without you. You are my one and only true love.

To my miracle babies, Holly Alexandra and Taylor Henry. You are the greatest gifts God has ever given me. My eyes light up every time I see you enter a room, and I am honored that I get to be your mum.

To Jesus. I am indebted to You forever. You have healed my heart and changed my life, and Your love has made me who I am today.

The dragonfly is a symbol of change—
a change in the perspective of how we see ourselves.
The dragonfly starts to grow in water . . .
and then it moves into the air to fly.
It pictures the transformation we experience when we
understand the deeper meaning of life.
Here's to seeing the change in you.

CONTENTS

FOREWORD

By Kari Jobe

Since buying a new home, I have enjoyed following interior decorating and style accounts on social media. I especially enjoy those that show before-and-after transformations where dated, mismatched, and cluttered spaces become fresh, clean, and inviting. In order for one of those spaces to become what the designer envisions, old patterns and styles have to be removed; the space must be decluttered, leaving a blank canvas onto which the designer can paint a new vision for the future.

That is the heart of this book. God has designed a way for each of us to live—one that is *Tailor Made* just for us. To arrive in that space, however, we sometimes have to allow God to remove the old in order to make room for the new.

Some people live in a place of breakthrough. When you see someone living freely, you want to know every detail of how they got there. Alex Seeley lives in such a place—one of breathtaking intimacy with the Father. When you see it, you can't help but desire the same level of depth and freedom in your own walk. To put it simply, once you taste that freedom, staying in your old place of brokenness and bondage is no longer an option.

When I first met Alex back in 2009 at a Hillsong Conference in Sydney, Australia, I was living out my dreams, traveling the globe as a worship leader. At that point, I had experienced a breakthrough from unhealthy patterns and bondage, but there were places in my heart where I had yet to fully experience freedom. In fact, some of those places felt like a tangled mess.

Throughout my life, God has graciously brought me into divine relationships at pivotal moments in my journey. As a twenty-eight-year-old looking for godly women to speak into my life, that encounter with Alex stirred my heart. She had kind eyes and was genuinely interested in my life.

As the conference came to a close, I worked up the courage to give Alex a copy of my first album. We laugh when we talk about it now, because I hardly ever just hand people my albums. But I found out later that the last track on that record, "You Are For Me," became a song God used in Alex's life during a difficult season.

Over the next few years, I ran into Alex at different events in both Australia and America. What I didn't realize then—but what I can see now—is that God was divinely connecting our paths. He was setting us up for a relationship that helped both of us experience the beauty of God-ordained friendship.

In 2014 I moved to Nashville, Tennessee, and began

attending a Tuesday night gathering in the basement of the Seeleys' house. Something started to shift for me in that basement. God began to touch my life in a fresh way. I love how the Lord used one of my songs in Alex's life to remind her of truth, because years later she turned it around and helped me walk out what it means to actually believe that truth in my own heart. It's amazing how God works! Alex has become a dear friend, and my husband, Cody, and I now call The Belonging Co. our church home. We are privileged to have Alex and Henry as our pastors.

Anyone who knows Henry and Alex Seeley is aware of their conviction to speak the truth in love. Sometimes that truth stings; it can feel uncomfortable. But when you know it's helping, you allow the Holy Spirit to move in a deep and life-changing way, and you can receive it. This book offers that kind of truth.

I promise you will feel seen and known as you read this book. The Holy Spirit will remind you of labels that were attached to you and of experiences that shifted your upbringing. But you will also feel the nearness and kindness of God's Spirit that helps you forgive, let go, break off, and move into a new mindset and new freedom—which is beautiful.

Alex has helped me navigate some of the deepest places of sorrow and pain I have experienced in my adult life. She understands her authority in Christ, and she has lovingly modeled for me the deeper places of healing that are freely offered to me as a child of God.

I remember one of these experiences like it was yesterday. It started when I received one of the hardest phone calls of my life. "Kari," said a broken and sorrowful voice on the other line. It was my seven-and-a-half-month pregnant sister Kris. "Kari," she continued, "James Ivy went to be with Jesus before we got to meet her." Then all I heard were quiet sobs on the other end of the line. As I wept with my sister, the experience of sharing her heartache began to uncover some deep wounds in my own heart—wounds that were connected with God. Through the years, I had begun to build up an offense toward God. The loss of my unborn niece felt like the straw that broke the camel's back.

A couple days after the funeral, I was scheduled to lead worship at a women's conference. But I felt mute. In my hurt, I felt so silenced that I couldn't find the words to pray, sing, or even speak. I was utterly heartbroken. I reached out to my dear friend Alex: "I need help navigating what's going on in my heart from this experience. I'm supposed to lead worship at the end of this week, but I can't even find my voice."

She wrote back immediately: "Just come over to my house. I've cleared my schedule."

I walked inside her front door and immediately just wept. We spent the day talking and unpacking where my heart was. She listened with compassion and helped me navigate deep places of pain, confusion, and disappointment. I had to repent of lies I believed; I had to replace those lies with truth from the Word of God. I also had to place my trust in Him again— trusting that He sees the bigger picture. Trusting that He is in control. Trusting that He works everything out for my good. It was a difficult process, but it was also sweet, tender, healing, raw, and real.

I've been blessed to know Alex Seeley as a friend, and I pray this book will multiply those blessings in your life.

As Alex unpacks her story, you will find practical insights and powerful prayers to help break generational curses and lies fed to us by the Enemy. We don't have to continue marching around with the same broken mess and hurt. God can reach deep into those places of trauma and disappointment and paint new pictures to replace them.

Just reading the first few pages of this book, I already had warm tears rolling down my face and a sweet knowledge in my heart that I was being invited into a journey of wholeness. It was a simple and peaceful invitation from God's Holy Spirit. He knows how and when to gently lead us into new places of freedom.

As you read this book, let the Holy Spirit highlight those spaces in your life He wants to heal. Let Him unlock you. Allow God to work within you as you read—He can change your belief system, change your confession, and deal with the unforgiveness deep within your heart, just as He did with me. We are *Tailor Made*. Each of us is living out a beautiful design.

I am so grateful for Alex and her honesty throughout these pages. I know you will be too.

—Kari Jobe

WHAT LABEL ARE
YOU WEARING?

Sticks and stones may break my bones,
but words will never break me.
—English children's rhyme

S ei cretina!"

    Sei cretina is Italian for "You're so stupid"—a label I wore for most of my life. This label shaped how I processed information and how I saw myself. My mum would use this phrase whenever I was clumsy, forgetful, gullible, or just plain naughty. Although the phrase was a cultural expression not meant to be cruel, it felt cruel. And I believed it.

    I recall one time when my mum gave me a task: "Alex, would you go to the store and buy a bag of frozen mint peas?" Simple enough, right? But by the time I walked to the store and found the frozen vegetable aisle, I had second-guessed myself and gotten confused on the instructions. Was it mint peas or green peas? My internal dialogue was filled with fear that I would make a mistake and get in trouble. The conversation in my mind went something like this: *Hold on a minute. Maybe she didn't say peas. Maybe I heard her wrong. Did she say beans? Oh no! I can't remember what she said! I'm going to be in so much trouble when I get home. Just get both so you cover all the bases. Wait, I don't have enough money to buy both.* . . . Panic and fear set in, as by this time I had been away long enough that I had to make a decision. I chose the green garden peas. All the way home I braced myself for a scolding because I was afraid I had chosen the wrong item. Over and over again I scolded myself: *Alex, you're so stupid. You're so stupid. You can't even do one simple task like buying a grocery item.*

I lived like this until my early twenties. I couldn't decide what I wanted to eat or what clothing I should buy. I changed my mind so many times that I worked myself into a frenzy—all because of the fear of making the wrong choice and being made to feel stupid.

Stupid was the label that I wore, but *stupid* I was not.

We all wear labels. Some labels we may choose, like Gap or Gucci. Others are given to us—labels that categorize and brand us with certain stereotypes, such as *beautiful, handsome, smart, athletic, creative, fat, stupid, ugly, clumsy,* and the list goes on.

Often the labels spoken over us by well-meaning people cause us to believe a lie about ourselves. We can allow one word or statement to box us in, and we end up living our lives restricted by a definition. No one enjoys being labeled or stereotyped.

Yet words can also be so good! There aren't enough adjectives in the English language to describe the many facets that make us unique.

You are an original. Not a copy of anything or anyone else. You were created with a fingerprint that no one else has. No two people on earth are exactly alike. Even identical twins have different fingerprints. If God went into such detail to imprint your fingertips, then don't you think He has an original design for your life that only *you* can fulfill? God's pattern for you is uniquely designed to perfectly match the abilities and talents He gave you.

God does not want us to wear any other label but His. In fact, He wants us to be such stunning masterpieces that people will either recognize our Designer's label or want to know what label we are wearing and how to get it too.

When God sees you, He sees greatness. He doesn't see ordinary. He sees extraordinary. Each of us has been tailor-made to reveal God's glory as individuals reflecting His nature. The term *tailor-made* means "fashioned to a particular taste, purpose, demand, etc."[1] or "perfectly meeting a particular purpose."[2] God gives us grace to fulfill what He has designed us to do. Grace is more than a free pass to heaven. It is God's enabling power that is sufficient, fit to size, and tailor-made just for you.

If you are wondering about your original design—or if you have ever asked, "Why am I here?", "Why was I born?", or "What is my purpose on this earth?"—let's take a closer look. The Master Tailor, our Designer, is extraordinary; therefore, we can be confident that we were also designed to be extraordinary. He tailor-made all of us to be one of a kind, created in His image, and destined for a master plan that He purposed before we were even born.

CHAPTER ONE

DESIGN OR ACCIDENT?

There are no *ordinary* people. You have
never talked to a mere mortal.
—C. S. Lewis, *The Weight of Glory*[1]

I'm an accident.

At least, that's the story I was told when I was growing up. One evening, when I was about five years old, I was sitting at the table enjoying dinner with my family, and my mum was sharing the stories about our family and how each of us came to be on this earth. It was always exciting hearing my mum tell a story. She has an amazing ability to make a story come to life. So much so that when I didn't want to eat my dinner, rather than argue with me she would begin to tell a story as she picked up the spoon to feed me. Her storytelling was so captivating that by the time she finished talking, I had eaten all my dinner without realizing it.

Each story my mum shared about my siblings that night was wonderful and filled with details of love and expectancy. I sat with eager anticipation, waiting for my story to be shared. After all, I was the baby of the family, and the best is saved for last. I remember my mum laughing as these words came out of her mouth: "Well, you were the accident that wasn't meant to happen!" The boys laughed and jeered along with her. My brother David added his own silly comment about how maybe I was actually adopted, joking that I didn't appear to have any resemblance to my parents. He also told me on many occasions, to annoy me and get a reaction, that he was the favorite and that my parents didn't love me as much as they loved him.

I laughed along with them because I wanted to feel included in this seemingly funny joke, but in reality I felt as if a knife had stabbed my heart. I felt rejected and unwanted. That day, I slowly began to deteriorate on the inside.

AN ITALIAN DRAMA

I was born on a Friday night in March—eight pounds, eight ounces of Italian goodness. Later, my mother told me that the doctor who delivered me made a point of saying, "This one is special," as she handed me to my mum. This was God's truth about me, but it took many years before I could see and believe it for myself.

There was no denying that I was the fourth child born into a family that had planned to have only two. My mum was quite vocal in reminding people—especially my father—about the original plan. But it was 1970, and they were raised Catholic. And Italian. So you can imagine how that went.

After the births of my sister and brother, my mum discovered she was pregnant again. After a near-death experience, she gave birth to my ten-pound brother David—and two children became three. Having three children was not ideal for my mother, but she decided to make the best of it.

Fast-forward a few years after David's birth. My sister had been praying and believing for a baby sister, and my mum went to the doctor to diagnose a mystery illness, which turned out to be . . . me. Surprise! The day she got the phone call with the results of her blood test, she passed out from shock. Like many 1970s housewives, she blamed my dad—because obviously, it was solely his fault. She refused to speak to him for three months. Don't you love Italian drama? When she finally started talking to him again, I'm sure it involved a lot of theatrical hand-waving and passionate arguing.

My mother once said to me something I will never forget. In the early months of finding out about me, she prayed that God would take me from her. One night when she was overwhelmed and crying out to God, she sensed the voice of the Lord clearly say, *This child you are carrying is Mine!* She didn't understand what that meant at the time, so she assumed that she was either going to die giving birth or that the child growing in her womb would die. Both scenarios overwhelmed her.

It wasn't that my mum hated kids. She didn't. It wasn't that she was being irrational. She wasn't. She had planned for two children, and in her mind, she could handle two children. But if her near-death experience giving birth to her third child wasn't terrifying enough, imagine the fear she must have felt thinking about giving birth to a fourth child. She told us that she stayed up many nights wondering if this fourth child would be her death. How would her husband care for four children on his own if she died? Or if she did survive this birth, how would she be able to take care of four children?

As the story unfolded that night around the dinner table, I was bewildered, to say the least. This was not the happy story I had expected. Instead, all I heard was that I was unplanned—an accident that made my mother's life miserable. I wanted to run to my room and cry into my pillow. I didn't know where to turn for comfort, because these words were coming from the very person who was supposed to be my comforter and nurturer. My mother had no idea, but that night a seed of rejection was planted into my soul—one I would struggle with for much of my life.

A FLAWED SELF-PERCEPTION

We all want to feel as though we belong in our families, so hearing that you are an accident is a tough pill to swallow. I didn't understand that it was an exaggerated statement at the time; as a young child, I took every word literally. Even though my parents loved me when I came into this world, the cruel and harsh truth was that they never wanted a fourth child.

I carried those words deep within my soul for a very long time. My self-perception was that I had no place in my family. Because I had been labeled an "accident," I chose to believe that I was anything but special.

We all listen to the voices that are spoken over us: "You are nothing," "You are stupid," "You are fat," or (in my case) "You are an accident." The popular children's saying "Sticks and stones may break my bones, but words will never break me" is a complete lie. Words cut through the heart and wound a person's spirit. The Bible says, "The tongue has the power of life and death" (Proverbs 18:21). We must choose our words wisely because they hold great power to hurt or to heal. Proverbs 12:18 reminds us, "The words of the reckless pierce like swords, but the tongue of the wise brings healing."

What I didn't know at the time was that my mum was carrying her own pain, resulting from struggles with her own mother. She had endured much disappointment over her lifetime, so she was a fractured person when she began to parent. As a result, she lived out the truth of the adage: "Hurt people hurt people."

My mum's angry outbursts and old-school discipline reinforced the message that I was a nuisance. Every negative word, outburst of anger, and harsh spanking became another brick that built on the foundation of "you are an accident." But my view of self went beyond how I thought my family felt about me. The mortar that held those bricks together consisted of an even deeper misunderstanding of God's love and plan for my life, combined with Satan's lies about my true identity. I had been taught in Sunday school that Jesus loved me, but what about the Father? Was it just His duty to love me because Jesus did? I thought surely God was not concerned with the details of my life or the reason I was placed on earth. I figured He was far too busy taking care of everyone else in the world to care about me, because other people deserved His attention more than I did. I felt unworthy in His presence. I viewed God as far away, sitting on a throne at a distance, waiting to punish people who were bad—people like me.

I remember a time when my mum lost her temper and lashed out at me. After she had finished yelling at me, she left the room without resolving the issue. I cried until I had a headache. I wondered what I had done to deserve such harsh punishment. I prayed to God and asked Him: "Why did You place me in this family? If You are a loving God, then why can't You tell my mum to stop?" After each outburst of anger, my mum would give me the silent treatment for hours, sometimes days, which reinforced the rejection I felt about being an unwanted mistake. Her anger and coldness caused me to feel deep shame, which further made me feel ugly and unlovable.

Because I felt ugly and unlovable, that self-perception became the filter through which I lived my life. I wanted to become invisible, because I was afraid that anything I did or said would trigger my mother's anger and lead to severe consequences. I felt as if I had to tiptoe through my home—as if there were land mines underground that would explode if I stepped on them. When I was with my friends or extended family, I went with the flow because I hated conflict and feared anyone getting angry with me. I would agree with people, even if I didn't truly agree with or like them. If they said they didn't like something, I would say, "Me too," even if it wasn't true.

My two cousins loved music. Their favorite bands were U2 and Adam and the Ants. (I grew up in the 1980s.) Once they asked me who my favorite band was, and I was too afraid to say anything, worried that if I mentioned a band they didn't like, they would mock me. So to avoid conflict, I simply said, "I don't have a favorite band." They couldn't believe it.

"How can you not have a favorite band?"

I said to them, "Well, you pick one for me." They were delighted with this suggestion! They thought for a few minutes, hashed out some ideas, and concluded that I should love Spandau Ballet—a popular English band at the time. *Spandau Ballet?* I thought. *I don't want them to be my favorite band.* The truth was, I wanted U2 to be my favorite because I loved Larry Mullen Jr., the drummer. But I didn't want to rock the boat because one of my cousins had already claimed U2 as her own. So I lied and said, "That's a great idea!" just to keep the peace. I know this might sound silly to you—as it does to me now—but that is how deeply affected I was. To please my cousins, I pretended for years that Spandau Ballet was my favorite band.

As I grew up, I became a first-class people-pleaser because I was starved for verbal affirmation. I thought trying to be accepted and refusing to disagree with anyone would distract from the fact that I was an accident. My heart was crying out for someone to validate me and tell me I was worthy of love, acceptance, and purpose simply because I was Alex.

Ironically, when anyone did compliment me, I didn't receive it as truth. Instead, their words ricocheted off the brick wall I had built around my heart. After feeling unworthy for so many years, I had put up strong defenses in an attempt to protect my heart from any future hurt. I let others lead me and tell me what to think because I believed my opinion didn't matter. I couldn't make decisions because I feared making the wrong ones and being judged for it. I told lies to convince people my life was better than it really was. Simply put, I was an internal mess who worked hard day after day to keep up the false exterior that I was okay. My façade said I was like every other girl.

ONE SIZE DOESN'T FIT ALL

From the moment we enter this world, we are surrounded by labels—words that discourage and disable us, words that degrade and devalue us, words that destroy our purpose in life. Some voices offer encouragement, but there are plenty more that discourage us. And we remember the negative words spoken over us so much more than the positive words given to us. Perhaps you had to bear a nickname like "the black sheep" or "nerd." Perhaps your mother said, "You're just like your father," whenever you were a nuisance to her. Maybe you were given another kind of label that put you in a box.

From the time Adam was created, there has been a target on humanity—Satan's well-executed plan to steal, kill, and destroy the people of God (John 10:10). According to Satan's one-size-fits-all plan, everyone is a target. If you are breathing, you are a target. The Enemy has one plan for everyone on earth, and it is this: to rob you of your purpose and to rip away your God-given destiny. He hates you in a bitter, jealous, raging, malicious way. He hates who you are, what you have, what you are entitled to, and who you have the potential to become. He hates that you are loved by God, and with a relentless jealousy, he hates that you are created in God's image. You remind him of everything he lost, and as a result, he has a strategic plan to destroy you.

What negative labels do you find yourself wearing? Every negative word spoken over you is part of Satan's plan—a lie from the Enemy. Satan's opposition to the truth is meant to antagonize and mock you. He sows seeds of discontent, saying, "You are not meant to be here," "You will never amount to anything," or, "People will only love you if you are successful." When you begin to believe these lies, the core of your belief system becomes founded on self-doubt. Satan undermines your dreams and diminishes your hope for the future through intimidation and fear—this is the force behind his one-size-fits-all plan to ruin your life and everyone else's lives too. He wants you to believe the lies spoken over you, making you believe yourself incapable of achieving the tailor-made plan that God has already designed for you.

You may have a fairy-tale story of how your parents prayed for you before you were conceived, planned for your entry into this world, and welcomed you with open arms. Or you might be the result of a one-night stand, a rape, or a surprise, as I was. Perhaps you were born and given away because, for a variety of painful reasons, your mother could not keep you or your father abandoned you at birth. Whatever the story of your origin, you can know this: God is the master Designer and divine Creator of the universe, and He has a tailor-made plan for you. Before time began, He designed a specific purpose that only you can fulfill. Jeremiah 1:5 says, "Before I formed you in the womb I knew you, before you were born I set you apart." You are not one-size-fits-all; you are tailor-made by the Designer of the universe.

God's plan for your life may be under attack. You may think your start in life was hijacked, or you may think your life has no plan at all. However, God's plan is greater than the Enemy's lie, because God's plan for you is strategic—not one-size-fits-all. God has a perfect, unique plan for good that has been tailor-made just for you. Even though Satan attacked His design, God will do whatever it takes to restore what Satan defiled in order to bring us back to His original design and purpose. He is a patient and masterful Designer who knows that anything of value takes time to construct. The details of a plan demonstrate the quality of the workmanship; therefore, it may require some time to restore you to God's intended design. But God always finishes what He starts.

Your start in life may not have been ideal, and you may be wondering why on earth you are here. I can assure you that once you discover who your God is, how much He loves you and desires relationship with you, and what He has planned for your life, you will also discover the reason you are here at this specific time and what you are meant to do. You are not an accident; you were lovingly designed by God, who has tailor-made a purpose for your life.

Why don't you take a minute and ask God to help reveal the areas in your heart that need healing? Allow Him to speak truth over your life to replace the lies you have believed.

Dear Lord,

Open the eyes of my heart and reveal the areas that need healing as I read through these pages. I want to hear Your truth. Wipe out the lies I have believed, and teach me to trust what You say about me. Speak to me and help me discover who I truly am.

In Your name, amen.

CHAPTER TWO

THE ORIGINAL DESIGN AND HOW IT BECAME FLAWED

God saw all that he had made, and it was very good.
—Genesis 1:31

I was born into an immigrant family. My father, Carmine, moved from Naples, Italy, in 1955 at the age of nineteen. With a small suitcase and the equivalent of twenty-five dollars in his pocket, he embarked on a journey for a better life than the one he left behind. He arrived on Australian soil not speaking a word of English. He had no job and no family. I can't even imagine what that must have been like for him.

My mum was also nineteen years old when she arrived in Australia, eight years later. My mum lived with her married older brother, whose wife happened to have a brother named Carmine. You guessed it—his wife's brother was the man who would eventually become my dad.

My mum was not at all thrilled about the living arrangements. My dad owned the home, and in true Italian tradition, they fit as many people as possible into the house to save money. My mother also couldn't speak any English, and she found the transition difficult because many of the natives in Australia treated immigrants with disdain and suspicion. To add insult to injury, she was living in a house with her brother, who was overbearingly protective and watched over her every move.

My father thought all his Christmases had come at once with this beautiful young woman living under his roof. So he did what all 1960s gentlemen did and asked her to marry him as soon as he had the chance. As my mum tells it, she wasn't in love with him—but she convinced herself that he was her ticket for freedom. She thought: *Well, Carmine is a good provider and an honest man who will love me and take care of me. Perhaps I can grow to love him.*

After my dad had asked her several times, one morning he said to her, "I'm not a beggar, so I won't ask again—but do you want to marry me?" She took a pen and wrote YES on the second page of the newspaper. Then she gave the paper to my dad and said: "Here you go. What does the news say today?" He was elated beyond measure, but his bubble quickly burst when she proceeded to say: "You need to know the truth. I like you but am not in love with you. I will marry you if you still want me." He was so in love with her that he replied: "My love will be enough for the both of us, and someday you will love me. I know that for sure." It was not a great foundation to build a marriage on. This explains why there were so many cracks along the way that affected our entire family.

On June 13, 1964, my mum and dad married in Adelaide, Australia. At the time, my dad worked as an automotive production line worker, and my mum worked as a kitchen hand in a hotel downtown. As soon as they were married, my father—being a proud Italian man—suggested that my mum no longer work because her job gave the appearance that he was unable to provide for her. Even though she loved to work and loved being with people, she reluctantly submitted and stayed home. She was only twenty-one and was full of dreams and aspirations of adventure, but my father wanted to begin a family right away. After all, he had married later in life compared to the other men around him.

My father was twenty-eight and desperately wanted children, so thirteen months after their wedding date, my oldest sister was born. She was the apple of my father's eye. He loved her and couldn't get enough of her. My mum recalls that when my dad would come home from work, he would bypass her and make a beeline for the nursery to kiss and love on my sister. My mum would tell me this story often, and even though she wasn't telling it to make me feel bad, somehow this story made me feel as if my dad loved my sister more than me. My heart was wounded because I believed I was a mistake. This couldn't have been further from the truth—my dad loved me—but I don't remember ever hearing a story about my dad being as besotted with me as he was with my sister. The truth is, it is normal for parents to hold every moment and memory of their first child as special, but that does not diminish how special their following children are to them. Again, the Enemy whispered a lie that built upon the foundation of his previous lies, which made me feel as if I was a reject and my family simply put up with me because they had no other choice.

The question of origin and to whom we belong goes deeper than our biology or our family tree. You might know who your biological parents are and love them dearly, or you might have a negative association with your parents due to the way you were brought up. Or, you may have had the best parents, yet you still lack a sense of belonging. I believe God designed us with a desire for belonging that only He can truly fulfill. So all of us, at some point in our lives, have felt like outsiders.

Beyond the burning desire to know *who* we are, we also need to know *why* we are here and *what* our purpose is. Yet no matter how many stories they tell us, our parents are unable to answer those questions fully. Even though they played an integral part in bringing us into this world, they did not have a complete plan for our lives that existed before we were born. God, however, did have a plan for us; He planned our lives before the foundations of the world. Ephesians 2:10 says, "We are God's handiwork, created in Christ Jesus to do good works, which God prepared in advance for us to do."

IN THE BEGINNING

Genesis 1 tells us that from the beginning, God had a plan. First, He created the heavens and the earth, the sun, moon, and stars, and everything that exists on planet Earth. He spoke it all into existence. He then completed creation by making humanity in His image. He gave the man and the woman dominion and authority over the earth. He gave them the power to rule over the animals and vegetation and the freedom to create and build a life. He told them to multiply and fill the earth with people who would worship and be in perfect relationship with Him. He created them with an individual purpose to fulfill and to release His glory, and He designed each of them uniquely. There was no sin, no pain, and no evil—just complete security, peace, and love. Life was exactly how God intended it to be.

We were created to live freely inside a loving relationship with the Father. The Bible says that God would walk with Adam and Eve in the cool of the day (Genesis 3:8). For a time, a perfect relationship existed between God and humanity. They were the first man and woman, yet they did not come out of a womb. They did not have an earthly mother and father. The only father they had was God Himself. His plan was to show them and teach them how to be a father and a mother, and they would follow His lead. Therefore, in the garden, God displayed His design for a perfect relationship with us. God created us not only so we could do things for Him—but more importantly, because He desired to have a relationship with us.

YOU WERE CHOSEN

There is something about being chosen that makes us feel quite special and included. Do you remember playing sports at recess in elementary school when two captains would pick their teams from the rest of the class? I remember what it felt like to be chosen first as part of the team. Being the first pick caused me to walk a little taller than everyone else. I would high-five the captain of the team and stand looking at the rest of the class as if I had just won the lottery. But when I was chosen last for a sport I wasn't good at, my shortcomings made me feel left out. That feeling was awful. It was embarrassing and shameful, because everyone knew what being picked last meant: you were not good enough, but you *had* to be chosen.

There is nothing worse than feeling as if someone is being forced to choose you. Our heavenly Father is not like that. He doesn't line us up to rank His "team" from first to last. The Bible says, "The last will be first, and the first will be last" (Matthew 20:16). God shakes up the natural system of being rewarded according to one's works. He doesn't operate in a merit-based system. He is generous, and He loves all His children. In fact, He chose us "while we were still sinners" (Romans 5:8) and then seated us in the heavenly realms with Him (Ephesians 2:6). Whether you have been a Christian since childhood or you confess your sin to Him on your deathbed, you were chosen to be in relationship with Him.

God designed us to worship and proclaim His goodness on earth and for all eternity. First Peter 2:9 says that we have been *chosen*, or set apart, to "declare the praises of him who called you out of darkness into his wonderful light." Ephesians 1:4–5 says: "He chose us in him before the creation of the world to be holy and blameless in his sight. In love he predestined us for adoption to sonship through Jesus Christ, in accordance with his pleasure and will." You—yes, you, reading this book—you were chosen by God, the Creator of the universe and all that is in it. You were chosen individually. You were chosen before He created any of it.

YOU ARE UNIQUE

You are one of a kind, unique among everyone else on the planet. There are approximately seven billion people on the earth today, and no two are exactly alike. No one in the history of the world has ever been exactly like you! You were marked for uniqueness to do something that no one else can do. We all have an individual fingerprint, tongue print, and footprint, which means we were each called to touch people's lives like no one else, to speak like no one else, to walk a path like no one else—and to leave a mark on this earth like no one else.

My friend Lisa Bevere once preached at a conference I attended, and she said, "God does not love His children equally." As she paused, I questioned her statement, thinking, *What? Of course He loves us equally. All men are created equal.* Then she proceeded with her statement: "God loves His children *uniquely*."[1] Then it hit me; *That is so true! What a revelation.* I felt God whisper in my heart at that very moment, *That is why when you pray and spend time with Me, you feel as though you are My most favored daughter.* When I spend time with Him, I feel as if I'm receiving His undivided attention—as if God loves me more than anyone else.

Too many of us are too insecure and afraid to stand out and be unique, so we never allow the expression of God's unlimited creativity to be expressed through us. We were designed to have a free and secure heart. When we are secure in our purpose and identity, this allows us and others to be all we were designed to be.

WHEN THE ORIGINAL DESIGN BECAME FLAWED

I once heard a story—perhaps a true story, or maybe an urban legend—that illustrates what I am about to say. There was a man who was stranded on the side of the road trying to fix his car, a Model T Ford that had broken down. While he was trying to fix the problem under the hood, a limousine pulled over, and a sharply dressed man stepped out. The man asked if he could look under the hood to see what the problem was. After tinkering with the engine, he asked the driver to turn the key and start the vehicle. The driver was a little taken aback, but any help at this point was gladly received. He went to the driver's seat, turned the key, and the vehicle started immediately. The man asked the gentlemen in the tuxedo, "Sir, why would someone like you stop to help someone like me?" The gentleman replied: "I'm Henry Ford. I created that vehicle, and it wasn't doing what I designed it to do. Because I designed it, I knew how to fix it." The driver could not believe it. The designer himself had fixed his car![2]

What about our human design? If we were created in the image of God, then how did the design become flawed?

Everything God created *was* perfect, but in His desire for true relationship, God added one unique characteristic to human design: the ability for us to make our own choices. He gave Adam and Eve free will—the option of living however they thought was best and right for them—because He wanted them to be free to make their own decisions, not to simply follow orders like robots. That ability to choose for themselves was tested when Satan took the form of a serpent and began speaking to Eve, questioning her understanding of God's nature and original plan (Genesis 3:1).

Satan will often use something or someone we are familiar with to deceive us and hurt us. If he didn't, we would recognize him immediately. He may also use our thoughts, planting lies in the very areas he knows we are weak and whispering negative thoughts to wound and confuse us. He will use that familiar and trusted person or thing to sow doubt and speak lies. Remember, he is the father of lies. He will twist a half-truth and form it into a big fat lie, just as he did with me by convincing me I was unwanted and unloved.

The Enemy has only one plan for my life, and it is the exact same plan he has for your life. Satan's plan is one-size-fits-all, for every person on this earth: to kill our identity and to steal our self-worth so that he can destroy our future. Do you see the strategy? Mess with a person's origins, and you corrupt their whole story. This is the reason why no matter what you do or how hard you try, the sum of all your striving and best efforts still equates to feeling *incomplete*.

The fall of man was initiated when Adam and Eve chose to believe a lie. The Enemy placed a seed of doubt in their minds and began a conversation with a simple question: "Did God really say, 'You must not eat from any tree in the garden'?" (Genesis 3:1). Notice that he went to the extreme and misrepresented what God said. Of course they could eat from other trees, but Satan just wanted to engage them in conversation in order to begin his deceitful manipulation. The same is true for us: Satan will use a truth and twist it to bring confusion. Before we know it, we are second-guessing everything and wondering what the truth is.

God said to Adam, "You are free to eat from any tree in the garden; but you must not eat from the tree of the knowledge of good and evil, for when you eat from it you will certainly die" (Genesis 2:16–17). The command was clear; there were no gray areas. So Eve responded to the serpent, "We may eat fruit from the trees in the garden, but God did say, 'You must not eat fruit from the tree that is in the middle of the garden, and you must not touch it, or you will die'" (Genesis 3:2–3).

The Enemy came in with a straight lie: "You will not certainly die . . . For God knows that when you eat from it your eyes will be opened, and you will be like God, knowing good and evil" (vv. 4–5). At that moment, Eve must have thought, *Well, this fruit does look pretty good, and I could get more wisdom if I eat it.* She began to look for what she thought she didn't have, not understanding that being made in the likeness of God, she already had wisdom inside of her. God was protecting Adam and Eve from knowledge that was evil and harmful to them.

THE RESULTS OF CHOICE

God placed that tree in the garden to offer Adam and Eve the ability to choose for themselves. But He also wanted to protect them, so He gave them instructions to stay away from it.

The Enemy went on with his twisted truth and led Eve to believe that God was holding out on her. He hinted that maybe there was something more—that she was missing out. The Enemy's one-size-fits-all strategy is the same for us today. He makes us believe that God is not as good as He says He is. I have often held a distorted view of God, wondering if He is withholding something from me because maybe He is disappointed with me or He favors someone else. This is a problematic, distorted view of who our Father is. This lie caused sin to enter the world, and as a result, people from that day forward would live separated from God, corrupting His original design.

This was the Enemy's plan all along. Satan knows your potential, because before he fell from heaven, he was an angel named Lucifer—the worship leader of heaven. He understood the power of God. He coveted that power and wanted to be like God. He once resided in heaven and saw every detail of glory. He wanted to be greater than God, but no one can be greater than God. Therefore, God cast him out of heaven.

When Satan saw that God made man in His image, he was furious. Can you imagine how angry that would have made him? Satan wanted to be like God, was thrown out of heaven for even thinking he *could* be like God—and there God was, creating man and woman to be like Him.

So Satan has been jealous of you since the day God breathed His spirit into you. Satan is on a mission to destroy your identity, to destroy the core understanding of who you are. He knows that because you are made in God's image, you are more powerful than any angel. If Satan can destroy your relationship with God and distort your view of Him, then his lies will affect the way you see yourself. Your default will become a negative self-image, where you highlight your weaknesses over your strengths—causing you to live an ordinary life that does not live up to the potential you were created and designed to live.

Dear Lord,

Help me to recognize and rebuke Satan's lies. Fill me with the truth of Your Word and the knowledge that You created me in Your image, for Your purpose. Thank You for Your desire to have a relationship with me. Create in me a free and secure heart as I discover and develop the purpose You have for me.

In Your name, amen.

CHAPTER THREE

THE FALLOUT FROM THE FALL

Sin entered the world through one man, and
death through sin, and in this way death
came to all people, because all sinned.
—Romans 5:12

G rowing up in my home, if I did what my mum and dad
expected of me, then all was well. But if I disappointed
them in some way, then I received the silent treatment for
days. I remember a time when I was in my junior year of high
school and brought home my report card. I had received all
A's and one C. When my mum looked at the report card and
saw the C for English, she looked at me with disappointment.
She ripped the report card in two and told me that I would
never amount to anything—that I might as well drop out of

school and work an average job that required no skill or intelligence. I felt crushed. I stood there in disbelief. *Did she just rip up my report card for getting one C?* I didn't know what to do, because if I pushed back and tried to explain myself, it would not have ended well. All I could do was punish myself in my mind and tell myself again how stupid I was.

Years later, I realized that my mum was desperate for me to succeed because she never had the opportunity to go to school beyond the fifth grade. She saw me taking for granted the education she had so desperately wanted for herself. While she thought she was challenging me to be better, what I heard was that I wasn't good enough and that I was stupid, which led me to feel unloved by her. This style of parenting wasn't just directed only at me; it happened with all my siblings. If we did not live up to my mother's expectations, then we often found ourselves on the receiving end of negative words and the silent treatment, which caused us to feel rejected and unworthy. To my mum's defense, this is how she had been brought up. As a result of her own mother's harsh criticism, she was pushed to work even harder. When she did the same thing to me, I understood her love as conditional—which made me feel as if God had conditions on His love too.

ALL YOU NEED IS LOVE

God designed us to be perfectly suited to have a loving relationship with Him. In the garden of Eden, Adam and Eve could freely give and receive love from God and from each other. However, God knew that a perfect relationship must also include the ability to make one's own choices, so He gave us free will. As we saw earlier, Satan manipulated Adam and Eve, and as a result of their choice to disobey God, sin entered the world.

After the fall, God's original design for us became flawed. Now, our design has some issues that need to be addressed. This is the fallout from the fall: We don't feel loved, and we don't see ourselves as God sees us. We believe Satan's lies and think we have to *be* good enough or *do* good enough in order to earn God's love.

But unlike many of our earthly parents, our everlasting Father does not operate on a point-and-reward system. He rewards those who diligently seek Him (Hebrews 11:6), not those who diligently do good works for Him. God will never be conditional in His love because He is love. He doesn't just feel love or give love. His very nature is love. The Bible is clear that nothing could ever stop God's love: "Neither death nor life, neither angels nor demons, neither the present nor the future, nor any powers, neither height nor depth, nor anything else in all creation, will be able to separate us from the love of God that is in Christ Jesus our Lord" (Romans 8:38–39).

God's approval of us precedes anything we have ever done, or could do, for Him. He loved us before we were even created. We had done nothing to earn His love. He loved us because we were His.

Our Father loves us because He made us. We are His beloved children. He loved us while we were yet sinners (Romans 5:8). He first loved us just because (1 John 4:19). He is love (1 John 4:8).

In Isaiah 43:6–7, God says, "Bring my sons from afar and

my daughters from the ends of the earth—everyone who is called by my name, whom I created for my glory, whom I formed and made.' The truth is clear: God made you for His glory, and He designed you to be like Him. He designed your every detail to be unique in form and function. Every characteristic and fiber of your being has meaning and purpose. God was at work in the secret place where no one but Himself witnessed you being formed (Psalm 139:15). He already knew you before you even took your first breath (Jeremiah 1:5). He was preparing you for the big reveal at birth.

SEEING OURSELVES AS GOD SEES US

For many years, I struggled to believe that God had a perfect design for me. As I got older, I became increasingly uncomfortable with my changing body. I was an Italian girl growing up in Australia, where most of the girls were blonde and blue-eyed. For some reason, those features were prettier to me. I had thick, curly black hair that, when I let it out, looked like Diana Ross and all the Supremes put together. Combing out those tangles was a nightmare. I used to stare at the mirror and tell myself how ugly I was and pull my hair out from the roots to punish myself.

I remember wishing someone would break my nose so I would have an excuse to have a rhinoplasty. I was already feeling awkward in my preteen body, but to add insult to injury, my mum would often say, "Be careful not to eat too much; it will make you large and unattractive." Wow! Just like that, Satan's lie began to stain my mind. I vowed to never let myself get big, because I was convinced I would be unacceptable and unlovable if I did.

I believed Satan's lie. He said if I could make the outside of my body perfect, then I would be acceptable to those around me. Preoccupied with how perfect my body needed to be, I became obsessed with what I ate and how I could reverse what I had just eaten. For years, I struggled with my body image. There were times I would be in conversation with people and look as if I were listening, when in fact, I was mentally calculating calories and planning a new strategy of starvation. The thinner I was, the more affirmation I received from those around me. I became addicted to the verbal affirmation about my outward appearance, which fueled the eating disorder that dictated my life. [I was so starved for affirmation and validation that I starved my physical body to obtain what I thought would bring me joy.] But it was exhausting and never brought me the security I was longing for.

Why do we try to reach an unattainable goal of outward perfection? Because somewhere along the way, we have bought into Satan's lie that our bodies are flawed and that in order to be loved, we need to make our bodies look perfect. Plastic surgeons are laughing all the way to the bank because of this very lie. Many people are unhappy with their exterior and truly believe if they can look a certain way, then they will be fulfilled.

During those years I certainly was not happy with my design. I had a long list of issues with how God made me. I thought my design was flawed and wondered why God made me unattractive and other girls beautiful. I was so focused on the exterior that I missed the fact that God had tailor-made me from the inside out—and that what He made was very good. He doesn't make mistakes.

God designed me to be unique from the other girls, not to conform to the one-size-fits-all ideal that Satan tries to deceive us into thinking we must achieve. However, all I cared about was what I was *supposed* to look like according to what the girls in my classroom and the magazines said I should look like. It made perfect sense in my mind that if I somehow achieved physical beauty on the outside, then my life would automatically be beautiful on the inside and all my problems would dissolve.

What I didn't realize while growing up was that I was broken and bruised on the inside—which was why I felt so ugly on the outside. Until I came to the realization that God needed to come into my heart and fix what was broken, I was continually chasing a false reality of outward perfection.

So for years, I struggled with rejection and body image issues. I rationalized and justified my behavior, unwilling to admit what was really going on. I hid behind lies and excuses for my eating disorder because I was afraid that if I shared the truth with anyone, they would reject and judge me, I couldn't bear the possibility of being rejected again. I lived in constant turmoil. I tried in my own way to be free, but I couldn't seem to gain freedom in the areas of body image and acceptance. I would stare at myself in the mirror, spewing words over myself: "You're disgusting." "You're fat." "How can anyone even stand to look at you?" On and on went the verbal abuse.

My heart was so wounded by the words that had been spoken over me as a child that I continually reinforced every word about how ugly I was. I put on a fantastic façade, one that could have earned me an Oscar. I convinced everyone around me that I was free when I really wasn't.

TRUE BEAUTY

In the fifth grade, we would often sit on the carpet at the front of the classroom and sing songs or listen as the teacher shared a story. On the ledge in front of us was a blackboard featuring a mission box with Mother Teresa's face. Below her, the caption read: "Give until it hurts." I was moved every time I looked at her face. There was something about Mother Teresa's eyes that conveyed pure love. They were strong yet gentle. I would get lost looking at that picture of her.

If I ever had money in my pocket to buy candy at the school canteen, I would be convicted about my sugary purchase at the sight of her. Thus, I would give every penny I had to the mission box instead. I admired Mother Teresa and longed to meet her one day. She was a celebrity in my eyes, yet she was not glamorous or fashionable. In fact, she wore the same, simple outfit day in and day out: a white sari with two navy blue lines around the trim. The cut was modeled from an Indian sari, simple and understated. Mother Teresa did not maintain the latest trends or wear expensive designer labels, yet she was an icon. Everyone in the world respected her, not for her fashion sense but for the beauty of her selflessness and service to others.

In the summer of 1987, my parents and I took a trip to Italy to visit our extended family. When we arrived in Rome, we were welcomed by two of my cousins, who were police detectives. Instead of going through the customs line with the rest of the passengers, we were ushered into a room where dignitaries and VIPs cleared customs. To my amazement, I saw a tiny, elderly woman standing there wearing a white sari with blue stripes on the trim. It was Mother Teresa! There I was, right in front of her—starstruck, to say the least. I only had enough courage to say a quiet "hello," and she politely replied the same. As she bowed her head and walked graciously away, I was forever impacted by her presence. There was strength in the way she carried herself. She was *beautiful*. Her sun-parched, weathered skin, wrapped up in a white sari, was not what most people consider fashionable. Yet all I could see was her radiant beauty. Mother Teresa was a perfect reminder that true beauty comes from within, and that an encounter with such beauty can make a significant impact on many people's lives.

THE BEAUTY OF OUR SPIRITS

Are you striving for beauty, the way I was for so many years? Know that the content of your heart is the true source of beauty, and that beauty can only come when we love ourselves and are comfortable in our own skin. When we understand what our Designer says about us and how He truly sees us, then the rest will fall into place. We need to teach our children how to realize the unique beauty they possess.

Beauty has nothing to do with makeup or hairstyles, but it has everything to do with your spirit and the content of your heart. First Peter 3:3–4 says: "Your beauty should not come from outward adornment, such as elaborate hairstyles and the wearing of gold jewelry or fine clothes. Rather, it should be that of your inner self, the unfading beauty of a gentle and quiet spirit, which is of great worth in God's sight." A gentle and quiet spirit describes a person who is humble, unpretentious, and unassuming. It is a person who shows kindness and love, putting aside selfish interests for the good of others. The inner beauty that the Bible describes comes from understanding that God, the Creator of the universe, carefully designed you and put you together. He did not just throw you together as an afterthought. You were meticulously designed by a Master Tailor who had very specific intention in the details of your design.

Our beauty resides inside our spirits; therefore, it doesn't matter how old we are because our true beauty will never fade. Our spirits are ageless. When your spirit is connected to God's spirit, your beauty is most visible.

Your spirit is what makes you a unique person. You can see this clearly if you watch someone pass away, as I experienced when my dad went to heaven. After my dad took his last breath, I stood next to him and couldn't believe how different he looked from a moment ago when he was still breathing. I realized that it was my dad's spirit that made him who he was. His body was just a temporary suit that he wore while on earth. His spirit is present in heaven right now, and that is what matters the most. Our spirits are what we take with us.

We spend far too much time trying to perfect our outward shells instead of getting to know how to develop our spirits, which is what makes a person truly beautiful. The Bible tells us in Galatians 5:22–23 that the fruit of God's Spirit is "love, joy, peace, forbearance, kindness, goodness, faithfulness, gentleness and self-control." When we demonstrate this fruit in our spirits, then the essence of God's beauty shines through us. This kind of beauty is undeniable and never fading—the definition of true beauty.

GOD'S ORIGINAL PLAN

By sending Jesus, God's plan was to restore our relationship with Him back to its original design before the fall. He never intended to be separated from us. He would not have gone to such great lengths in giving up His own Son if He didn't want relationship with us. The relationship we broke, God restored. His desire has always been *you*! He made you perfectly, and there is no flaw in you.

The following list explains our spiritual inheritance and describes the original design God intended us to walk in.

Significance

If you search the entire Bible, you will not find the word *insignificant* when it comes to describing you. You are worthy, which makes you significant. You are important because you belong to God. You are His child, and that makes you significant. The Bible calls us God's heirs (Romans 8:17). We have an inheritance that is eternal (Hebrews 9:15). We are precious in the eyes of God, and He loves us (Isaiah 43:4). It's time you stop seeing yourself as insignificant and know that you are significant because God created you—and because there is only one of you.

Authority

In the garden of Eden, God gave humanity authority and dominion over the earth (Genesis 1:26). Even though we handed over our authority and gave it to the Enemy through our disobedience, Jesus came to make right what we did wrong. Because of His blood we are now made righteous in Christ Jesus. His purpose was to repair our broken relationship with the Father so we might receive authority "to overcome all the power of the enemy" (Luke 10:19).

Security

There was no such thing as insecurity in the garden of Eden. Humanity lost their sense of security when sin entered their hearts. Adam and Eve hid from God because they realized they were naked and felt shame and insecurity (Genesis 3:10). But Jesus came to reestablish our security and remove our shame by taking our place and dying on the cross; He displayed the greatest act of love by dying for our sins. We have a guarantee that He will never leave us nor forsake us (Hebrews 13:5). We can find complete security in our relationship with Jesus because God is our refuge and our strength. He is always available to us, in good times and also in times of trouble, so we can be secure in Him and we have no reason to be afraid (Psalm 46:1–2).

Relationship

God's desire has always been you. He created you not because He was lonely but because He wanted to reveal His glory through you. He wanted to share everything He had with us and to give us a rich and beautiful life that came out of the pure love He has for His children. His desire is for us to commune with Him without lack or dysfunction. Our perfect relationship with Him will then overflow, enabling us to have perfect relationships with one another as well.

Acceptance

When Adam and Eve sinned, they became separated from God. The consequence of their sin was spiritual death. But the love of the Father was so strong, even in that moment of disobedience, that God had already made provision for Jesus to come to us, take our punishment, reconcile us to the Father, and make it so we can be fully accepted as His children.

Freedom

My life verse is Galatians 5:1, which says: "It is for freedom that Christ has set us free. Stand firm, then, and do not let yourselves be burdened again by a yoke of slavery." When Jesus died in our place on the cross, He said, "It is finished" (John 19:30). No longer does sin need to be a yoke that enslaves you; now you can live in true freedom. The Bible assures us that "if the Son sets you free, you will be free indeed" (John 8:36).

Our original design is under attack by a real Enemy who came to steal what was not rightfully his. When sin entered the world, we inherited labels we were never designed to wear. Acceptance was replaced with rejection, innocence was replaced with shame, authority was replaced with weakness, dominion was replaced with insignificance, and security was replaced with insecurity. But the good news is that Jesus came to destroy the works of the evil one and to reestablish our position as sons and daughters of God.

You may be put together perfectly on the outside, yet still feel inadequate and incomplete. You may think you are ugly, as I used to. You may believe Satan's lie that you are not good enough. You need to understand that if you don't acknowledge how God put you together on the inside, then you will never fully grasp how valuable or beautiful you are. Beauty comes from within. Don't overcompensate superficially for what you feel you lack on the outside. Instead, draw from your understanding of how you were intentionally and perfectly tailor-made by God. Go directly to the Designer, who knows every facet of your being and every detail in your design, both physical and spiritual. Go to your Designer and consider how He put you together.

> *Dear Lord,*
>
> *I am sorry I have seen myself as flawed. I choose to believe that I have been uniquely designed and purposed to live in relationship with You. I repent for feeling unworthy and unlovable. I choose to believe the truth that I am fearfully and wonderfully made. Thank You for creating me from the inside out, and help me discover the true beauty that lives inside of me.*
>
> *In Your name, amen.*

CHAPTER FOUR

THE POWER OF A LABEL

The tongue has the power of life and death,
and those who love it will eat its fruit.
—Proverbs 18:21

A label in and of itself is not a bad thing. Labels help describe objects and people—something I once discovered can be very essential.

One day, as I got lost in the world of Pinterest, I saw pictures of pantries that looked like shop windows, which inspired me to update my pantry. I decided to go all Martha Stewart and take every item that was in a packet or box and place them, ingredient by ingredient, in clear mason jars. This included flour, salt, sugar, rice, oats, breakfast cereal, and everything else that would not look pretty if it wasn't in a jar.

I made a list of how many jars I needed, went to the store with great excitement, came home, and began the pantry transformation. I was so proud of myself when I looked at my pantry—everything lined up in rows and color-coordinated for an extra special touch. What I didn't realize is that self-rising flour and all-purpose flour look exactly the same, as do salt and sugar. In all my excitement, I had not thought about attaching labels to any of the jars. Cue my husband rolling his eyes at me as I write this story. He is the most organized person I know, and this would have been the first thing he would have done if he were updating our pantry. He would have designed labels and printed them after counting how many jars he needed.

When it came time to make a cake, I needed two cups of self-rising flour—but I couldn't tell which jar had the self-rising or the all-purpose flour. After all my hard work, I still had to go to the store and buy a bag of self-rising flour. If I had just labeled my jars, it would have made life so much easier.

Labels can be extremely helpful for identifying items in the pantry, but they can become equally dangerous when used to stereotype and box in a person. We all tend to live up to our descriptions—both positive and negative.

Some of us define who we are by what we do or who we have been told we are like. When asked, "Who are you?" most of us would say, "I am a parent," "I am a teacher," or "I am a spouse." Actually, these are not who we are; they are simple labels that describe what we do or who we are connected to. Perhaps you were labeled when someone said, "You are like your father" or "You are the class clown." Whatever the label, it forms how you see yourself, which in turn affects your behavior.

I knew a girl who was referred to by her parents as "the black sheep in the family." She was labeled the bad girl. The girl who always got in trouble. From a young age, she was wild and rebellious and could not be controlled by her parents. She became exactly what was spoken over her. It was easier to be who others said she was rather than fight to be anything else.

(handwritten margin note: having I am giving)
(handwritten margin note: what am I into?)

HOW LABELS DEFINE US

Growing up as an Italian in Australia was interesting. I was Italian by bloodline but Australian by birth and citizenship. Even though Australia was the only home I knew, I was considered a foreigner there. When I went back to Italy to visit extended family, I was seen as a foreigner there also. Where did I belong? I felt displaced everywhere I went. *Wog* is what I was called in Australia, and *Australiana* is what I was called in Italy. A *wog* is a term used for anybody from a Mediterranean background. It had an awful stigma to it. It meant "less than," "different," "outsider." When those words were spoken over me at school, I felt the harsh arrow piercing my identity, making me feel that I didn't measure up and that I had no place being there.

One day when I was walking along the sidewalk minding my own business, a woman shouted from a moving vehicle, "Go back to your own country, you wog!" After the initial shock of being yelled at by a stranger, those words sunk in and made me feel ashamed. I felt like I had been punched in the gut with those words. *Go back to my country? This is my country, and it says so on my birth certificate.*

Because of the cruel and harsh words that were spoken over me by people who never bothered to get to know me or hear my story, I was ashamed to be Italian. I allowed those words to shape my self-esteem. Was it because we looked different, we ate different foods, and our parents were not white-collar professionals? People fear what they don't understand, and then they label it with a definition that makes them feel better than those who are different.

The word *wog* sounded so harsh and cruel. When I heard it directed at me, it made me want to morph into someone else so I wouldn't be judged for my nationality. *How dare people stereotype me?* I thought. *I'm not like my parents. I shouldn't be judged by where I come from. I should be judged for the type of person I am.* People couldn't even work out whether I was Italian, Greek, or Lebanese—and to them, it was all the same anyway. So *wog* was the label I lived under for most of my adolescent and teenage years. Ashamed of my heritage, wishing at times that my parents had stayed in Italy so I would not have felt like an outsider, I tried my hardest to disassociate myself from my culture. I decided to be the most non-Italian girl possible. I made sure my speech was clear and articulate. I made sure I dressed fashionably and looked as non-Italian as I could. I put so much effort into something so futile because of those powerful, shameful words.

Not only did my own mother label me a mistake, but now I was labeled unwelcome in my community. I wondered if I belonged anywhere, which caused me to feel incredibly insecure about myself and put a big dent in my identity.

Labels usually begin at home during early childhood, as mine did. Being labeled an accident caused me to believe I was not meant to be here. Feeling as if I had no purpose or destiny then dictated how I functioned throughout my childhood.

In most families with siblings, you tend to get labeled according to your general personality traits. You may have been labeled "the pretty one," "the smart one," "the forgetful one," "the accident-prone one," "the rebel," "the responsible one," "the leader," "the follower," "the joker," "the glutton," "the black sheep," "the saint," "the fat one," "the tall one," "the musical one," "the genius" . . . and the list could go on and on. This label blankets your life whether you choose it or not. You become so used to hearing who someone else says you are that you never take the time to discover who you *truly* are. More importantly, you don't discover who *God* says you are.

No one's family is perfect, and sometimes parents play favorites. Parents with more than one child tend to label their children with certain attributes according to their perspectives. My mother gave each of us labels that we were required to live up to. My sister's labels were "responsible," "reliable," and "perfectionist." Mine were "dreamer," "forgetful," "lazy," and "unreliable," as well as "the accident" and "stupid." Because my mother saw me as less capable than my sister, I got away with things that my sister was punished for when she was my age. My sister was held to a high standard, but I was not. I was always making excuses and being excused. After all, I was the baby of the family, so I could slide under the radar. I was never seen as the one to rely on, so I became what was spoken over my life. I became lazy and forgetful around the house because I believed I was living up to my name.

Our parents have known us the longest, so of course they should know us best, right? No matter how well our parents might know us, they still view us through a veiled lens. Sometimes our parents want us to live the lives they were never able to achieve, so they decide who we are going to be early on.

FROM CUE BALL TO CUTE GIRL

When my friend Carol was a teenager, she decided to get her hair cut short. She couldn't wait to show her dad her new hairstyle, so she bounced into the room where her dad was. He looked at her and said; "You look like a cue ball. I'm not sure whether you look like a boy or girl." She was devastated and felt ugly and ashamed. She walked out of that room feeling like a deflated balloon.

Because those words pierced her heart and soul that day, Carol walked through her teenage years believing what had been spoken over her. That day affected how she saw herself and how she felt others saw her. Decades later, when she was an adult and had developed a personal and intimate relationship with Jesus, she spent time with Him and prayed a prayer that changed her life. After her experience, she wrote in her journal:

> Lord, You know that those words went down to the bedrock of my self-image. It opened a gateway for shame, insecurity, and self-hatred to come in. I picture those curses staining my soul like permanent black ink that kept swirling around until it permeated all areas of my self-image. I see now that there are still places that the black ink is causing darkness in areas of how I see myself.

Carol then wrote what she believed God was saying to her in response:

> I've been waiting for this moment for a long time. I know that when those words were spoken over you, it was very hurtful. It was like a stream of darkness blackening the light of who I designed you to be. That blackness coated your joy, so the only thing you could see was what the black represented. I know so much of the ink has been removed now, but there is still an inkblot from those words that are clouding your view. Climb up on My shoulders because I want to take you higher, to see yourself from a perspective other than your own.

Carol writes that her eyes were opened. She saw that even after many years, the dark spot was indeed still in her heart. Wondering why she couldn't rid herself of it, she sensed God speaking to her heart: *You didn't realize how much that one offhanded comment had affected your self-worth. I have been ready for you to bring it to Me for a long time.*

Carol was ready for complete healing. She envisioned Jesus laying His hand on her heart, and she watched as the inkblot started moving into His hand. She wondered if that was it, if the work was finished. Then again she sensed Jesus saying: *That's it! Now I want to fill the spot that has been in the dark for so long with My love for you. Do you know how crazy in love I am with you? You give Me so much joy. I love how you go with Me, without hesitation, on our adventures together. Don't ask why, but simply take hold of My hand—and off we go.*

Carol said in her dream Jesus opened His hand. The inkblot was there, only now the words looked completely different.

It went from "You look like a cue ball. I'm not sure whether you look like a boy or a girl" to "Boy, aren't you a cute girl. Didn't know if you would want to have a ball with me?" Notice that from the word *cue*, He placed His cross in it to become *cute*.

Carol wrote:

The word of man wounds, but the word of God heals. We must exchange negative words for life-giving words.

Wow! How amazing is that? The God of the universe rearranged the words that had wounded her self-esteem. Yet God made a new sentence from those ugly black spots that changed the original meaning into something beautiful.

HOW WE VIEW OTHERS

I have come across many beautiful people who have been saved by God's grace, but I have also seen the damage done to those same people because they have not been able to move past the labels they were given before they became Christians. People still view them as a product of their past. Sometimes it was the church people who were the most unforgiving.

I have seen drug addicts and prostitutes who were full of shame come to know Jesus. And I have seen professionals and prestigious people come to know Jesus as well. Some are successful in the eyes of society, and others are looked down upon because they are less fortunate; yet Jesus radically saves them all, and they begin to walk out their newfound freedom.

But even though God has removed their sin and given

them a fresh start, some people's family members and friends remember only the pain they caused and their past destructive behavior. In this way, saved people can carry a stigma, thinking what they've experienced won't last—because after all, a leopard never changes his spots. Once a drug addict, always a drug addict. Once a convicted felon, always a felon. Right?

I have watched some of these precious people try to live out their salvation with baby steps, only to find themselves still answering to the old labels that won't go away. I watch as they eventually go back to what was familiar, back to live their lives according to the labels they still carry in their hearts.

OVERCOME THE LABELS OF WHAT YOU ARE NOT

My husband has loved music since he was in diapers, dancing around the living room playing air guitar to the soundtrack of *Sesame Street*. His dream was to become a professional musician, and a professional musician is what he became. He is a prolific songwriter and worship leader who, at a young age, pioneered a sound of worship that has been released over many nations. He is known by his peers as a brilliant worship leader, musician, writer, producer, and a Grammy Award–winning mix engineer. In my opinion, the man is a genius, and everything he does is gold.

The label that was spoken over Henry's life was worship leader and gifted musician. And even though that is what he has done for his entire adult life, God also called him to expand his skill set and serve as a senior pastor of The Belonging Co. Church. "Senior Pastor." Henry did not see himself as a pastor, let alone a senior pastor. You see, he had been told for most of his ministry life that he was not a good leader and that he was not pastoral.

Sometimes the power in someone's tongue can be destructive. When people tell you what they think you are *not*, they box you into one area and hold you ransom to that one talent. So when it came time to lead the church, Henry was reluctant to lead and had to battle the lies in his mind that said he was not a leader and that he was not equipped to pastor a church. He would compare himself to other pastors across the nation and see his lack of ability against their incredible abilities. He would often tell me, "I am not that guy." He struggled with the noise that kept getting louder in his ear. But even though he may have not been man's idea of what a senior pastor looks like, God had other ideas. The Bible says that God uses the foolish things of this world to confound the wise (1 Corinthians 1:27), and throughout Scripture you will often see the most unlikely person having incredible favor and doing unbelievable things in order to give God the glory. After believing what God said about him and disabling the lie of what others had said he is not, Henry is now walking in the fullness of his calling. Not only is he still an incredible worship leader, but he is also a wonderful senior pastor.

You may have been labeled with words that make you feel less than. Maybe you have been told what you are not. Maybe you feel common, cheap, and ordinary because of what someone else has said about you. But God can take what others view as trash and transform it into the treasure He designed you to be. He can take what is broken and bruised and turn it into something beautiful. Isaiah 61:3 says that God will give "a crown of beauty instead of ashes, the oil of joy instead of mourning, and a garment of praise instead of a spirit of despair." What a beautiful picture! God takes our brokenness and makes something beautiful out of it, and then He places His seal upon us and marks us as His own.

The Bible says in 2 Corinthians 1:21–22 that God has "anointed us, set his seal of ownership on us, and put his Spirit in our hearts as a deposit, guaranteeing what is to come." The Spirit is the official seal—or Designer's label—of God's ownership, marking believers as His own and producing godly character in us.

Dear Lord,

Thank You for taking my brokenness and turning it into something beautiful. I confess that I have believed Satan's lies and have accepted his labels of shame and guilt for far too long. Today, I will peel off the labels of my past and proclaim the power of Your label, which transforms me into the treasure You designed me to be! May Your seal of the Holy Spirit demonstrate to others that I am Your own, and may You produce godly character in me.

In Your name, amen.

CHAPTER FIVE

HOW JESUS
CHANGES EVERYTHING

If anyone is in Christ, the new creation has
come: The old has gone, the new is here!
—2 Corinthians 5:17

Mark 5:1–20 is a story about a man who lived in a grave-yard. Everyone was afraid of him. His reputation was that he was insane. The Bible says he was demon-possessed. Night and day, he would cry out in torment and cut himself. I can't even imagine what a tortured soul he was. He could not coexist with society, so he had to live among the dead. Everyone kept as far away from him as possible due to their fear of him.

But when Jesus approached him from a distance, this demon-possessed man immediately ran toward Jesus and fell at His feet. It was the first time he had seen someone more powerful than what was inside of him. Jesus asked him, "What is your name?" The man replied, "My name is Legion, for we are many" (v. 9). This is how he was labeled by members of his society: demon-possessed. Insane. An outcast. A madman. The word *legion* means "a vast host." It was used to describe a multitude of Roman soldiers—or in this case, a multitude of demons.

When Jesus cast the demons out of the man, He gave them permission to enter a herd of pigs. The pigs, filled with those demons, ran off a cliff and drowned themselves in the lake. Legion was no longer. This man was healed and in his right mind!

When the people in this region of the Gerasenes saw what had happened, they were furious. They cared more about their pigs drowning than a tormented soul being set free. So they pleaded with Jesus to leave the region. They did not celebrate this man's freedom; in fact, they continued to fear him. This man wanted to leave and be with Jesus because his peers still labeled him as "insane."

Jesus told him, "Go home to your own people and tell them how much the Lord has done for you, and how he has had mercy on you" (v. 19). In other words, Jesus was saying: "These people may always see you as Legion, but I see you as My son. Now go and tell the people in the Decapolis what I have done for you." The man did as Jesus asked, and the Bible says, "all the people were amazed" (v. 20).

GOD-GIVEN LABELS

The Bible speaks of God's mercies being new every morning (Lamentations 3:22–23). We forget that if we truly repent, God in His faithfulness promises to remove our transgressions as far as the east is from the west (Psalm 103:12). He chooses to forget and remove our sins! Sadly, we often don't forget. Instead, we judge and label people by their past mistakes. In doing so, we make it hard for them to move forward in life.

We should be careful not to judge because Jesus warns us that the same measure we use to judge others will be used on us (Matthew 7:1–2). So often Christians are known for what we hate and stand against instead of what we are for, which is the saving power of Jesus Christ. His sacrifice causes us to be transformed into new creations. His gift to us is a clean slate.

Throughout the Bible, we see many labels placed on men and women of God who were viewed as anything but extraordinary. Yet when God encountered them, He called them by their God-given names. He took the label that was meant to hurt them and exchanged it with His label, which empowered them to be who He designed them to be.

- David was labeled by his family as the "youngest" and "the shepherd boy." He was overlooked by his own father when the prophet Samuel came to choose one of Jesse's children to be Israel's future king. But David was chosen by God and labeled "king of Israel" and "a man after God's own heart."
- Gideon labeled himself as the "least of his family," and

his clan was the weakest in Manasseh. Yet God named him a "mighty warrior." When Israel came under siege by the Midianites, it was Gideon who led the people into a great victory.

- Jacob was labeled as "supplanter" when he came out of the womb grabbing his twin brother's heel. Later he had an encounter with God, who wrestled with him. In that moment, God called him according to His purpose, not Jacob's present reality. God said, "Your name will no longer be Jacob, but Israel, because you have struggled with God and with humans and have overcome" (Genesis 32:28).

- Rahab was labeled a "prostitute" by the two spies who went to Jericho to spy out the land. But when she discerned that God had given the land to the Israelites, she made a deal that if she helped the spies, then they would take care of her and her family. Not only was Rahab spared, but she later married Salmon, who was a leader in the tribe of Judah (Num. 1:7; Ruth 4:20). Because of her faith, God labeled Rahab "family" and placed her in the lineage of Jesus Christ.

- The woman caught in adultery was labeled "condemned" by the Pharisees. They dragged her into the street and left her to stand there, possibly naked and judged by onlookers. But Jesus turned the situation around and said to them, "Let any one of you who is without sin be the first to throw a stone at her" (John 8:7). One by one those condemning her dropped their stones and walked away. Jesus looked in her eyes and said, "Has no one condemned you?" "No one, sir," she said. Jesus replied: "Then neither do I condemn you. Go now and leave your life of sin" (vv. 10–11). In other words, Jesus labeled her "clean" and told her to live in freedom.

- The woman with the issue of blood was labeled "unclean" and "outcast" because of a medical condition. Society gave her this label because of a situation that was out of her control. One day she heard Jesus was in town and said to herself, "If I just touch his clothes, I will be healed" (Mark 5:28). She touched his cloak, and immediately her bleeding stopped. Jesus knew at that moment that healing virtue had left His body, and He asked, "Who touched my clothes?" (v. 30). When she responded, Jesus looked at her and called her "daughter." He said: "Daughter, your faith has healed you. Go in peace and be freed from your suffering" (v. 34).

I was labeled a *wog*—a cruel and derogatory term for an outsider. I remember a night when I was scribbling on notepaper and writing the word *WOG* over and over. I looked at it with disdain and questioned why the world had to be so cruel. Then I felt a whisper in my heart that said, *Don't read it as a word; read it as an acronym.* I wrote "WOG." I sensed the Lord saying to me: *Do you know what that stands for? Woman of God!* Well, that changed everything for me. The very word that was intended to shame and box me in was now a phrase that redefined who I was. I wasn't limited to my nationality or even the name my parents gave me. I was called a "woman of God," and it made all the difference.

The power of a label can make or break you. Allow God to take the labels that have hurt you and exchange them for healing words.

God changed someone's name in each of these amazing stories. The name that circumstances or people had spoken over their lives no longer defined them after God's intervention. Throughout the Old Testament, a name carried significance. Whenever God gave a person a new name, it was to establish a new identity: "If anyone is in Christ, the new creation has come: The old has gone, the new is here!" (2 Corinthians 5:17). God gives us new names when we surrender our lives to Him. He labels us "heirs of God" and "adopted sons and daughters." You no longer have to bear the name that has been given to you or that you have labeled yourself with. Jesus is waiting to give His name to you.

CARRYING HIS NAME

We now wear His name as our label, and that holds priceless value. You are royalty. First Peter 2:9 says, "You are a chosen people, a royal priesthood, a holy nation, God's special possession, that you may declare the praises of him who called you out of darkness into his wonderful light." I have often heard the term "fashion royalty" used to describe certain designers who are at the top of their game. They are considered royalty because of how they rule the fashion world. We are heirs of the Designer of the universe, thus making us true royalty. We have been adopted into the family and now carry His name. We are tailor-made, and we wear the most important label of all.

These are some of the labels we now possess because we have been made in the image of God:

Generous

Our divine nature has been designed to be generous because our Father is generous. He is a good Father who lavishes His love, His provision, and His kindness on us. That's why it doesn't *feel* right to be stingy, to withhold, or to hoard, because even scientists have said that our brain releases endorphins when we give. Therefore, it truly is better to give than to receive (Acts 20:35).

Righteous

This doesn't mean self-righteous. Righteousness simply means having a heart that wants to do what is "right" in the eyes of God because it pleases Him. The law of God is written on every heart, and deep down we know what is right and what is wrong. When our heart is in love with Jesus, we want to do what is right in His eyes.

Creative

You are creative whether you can paint, play music, administrate systems, or build houses. Every person was designed to create and build, just like our Father. One of the first assignments He gave Adam in the garden was to name all the animals. God takes pleasure when we create something out of nothing because it reflects His creative nature (Genesis 1:1).

Beautiful

God makes everything beautiful. Isaiah 52:7 says, "How beautiful . . . are the feet of those who bring good news." David described the beauty of the Lord in Psalm 27:4: "One thing I ask from the LORD, this only do I seek: that I may dwell in the house of the Lord all the days of my life, to gaze on the beauty of the Lord and to seek him in his temple." If God is beautiful, then you and I—made in God's image— are also beautiful. Sin has made things ugly, but we were designed for beauty.

Faithful

God is not looking for those who are famous; He is looking for those who are faithful. God can use people who keep their word and stay the course by not giving up or taking the better offer. He is a faithful God who keeps "his covenant of love to a thousand generations of those who love him and keep his commandments" (Deuteronomy 7:9).

Alive

We may be breathing, but that doesn't mean we are fully alive. Being fully alive means living life to the full. A heart that is free can live an abundant life. Jesus did not come to earth and die on the cross so you could just exist until you get to heaven. He came to give us life "to the full" (John 10:10). And that means each one of us. Jesus is not dead. He is alive (Luke 24:5–6), and His resurrection power lives in you!

Loved

God is love, and the greatest desire of every person is to be loved and to be able to love. Love binds our hearts together and makes us feel like we belong. Love is what changes everything. It heals, restores, and unites. We all have the ability to love others, and it starts by receiving love from the One who loved us first.

Peaceful

The Bible says: "Do not be anxious about anything, but in every situation, by prayer and petition, with thanksgiving, present your requests to God. And the peace of God, which transcends all understanding, will guard your hearts and your minds in Christ Jesus" (Philippians 4:6–7). Therefore, we have the choice to be anxious or to pray with thanksgiving, casting our cares upon God and allowing the Prince of Peace to be our peace.

Patient

Patience is a virtue. It is virtue we all possess, yet many of us need to exercise it. Patience helps us grow into strong and resilient people. When we learn the art of being patient, we can fully trust that God is in control and that His timing is the perfect timing in all things. Second Peter 3:9 says, "The Lord is not slow in keeping his promise, as some understand slowness. Instead he is patient with you, not wanting anyone to perish, but everyone to come to repentance."

Kind

It's God's kindness that leads people to repentance (Romans 2:4). That means the world just needs more kindness shown to others. Kindness changes atmospheres. If each one of us were kind to one another, then our world would look very different. The Bible tells us: "Love your enemies, do good to them, and lend to them without expecting to get anything back. Then your reward will be great, and you will be children of the Most High, because he is kind to the ungrateful and wicked" (Luke 6:35). Kindness starts with us, and if someone is mean-spirited, we can choose to move in the opposite spirit to disarm the explosion that happens when we refuse to let go of our offense or our rights.

Good

When God created us, He said we were "very good" (Genesis 1:31). Sometimes when *good* is used as an adjective, we think it's less than great. But if God chose to use the word *good* for creating the universe and everything in it—including you—then the word *good* is good enough for me. Psalm 100:5 says, "For the LORD is good and his love endures forever; his faithfulness continues through all generations."

Gentle

A gentle spirit carries beauty and is valued in God's eyes. Beauty doesn't come from outside adornment but rather through gentleness. Jesus described Himself as gentle. He said, "I am gentle and humble in heart, and you will find rest for your souls" (Matthew 11:29).

Self-controlled

Because we are created in the image of God, we have self-control within us. Many of us just need to exercise this attribute. Imagine if we all decided to listen to that still, small voice of the Holy Spirit speaking to our hearts when we are about to do something negative. In that split second, if we can obey that tiny voice, then we won't have half the issues we have to deal with today.

As I wrote these out, I noticed that nine of those characteristics are commonly known as "the fruit of the Spirit," which is found in Galatians 5:22–23: "The fruit of the Spirit is love, joy, peace, forbearance, kindness, goodness, faithfulness, gentleness and self-control. Against such things there is no law." This fruit of the Spirit—the same Spirit who rose Jesus from the dead—becomes ours when we receive Jesus.

TO WEAR OR NOT TO WEAR: THAT IS THE QUESTION

When my husband and I were dating, we were invited to a wedding. I asked him if he owned a suit, and he said, "Yes, I do." I asked him to put it on so I could see how it looked. When he came out to show me, I didn't know whether to laugh or cry. He stood there in front of me with a suit two sizes too big. I asked him where he had found this suit. He said: "Oh, it's Johnny's suit that he let me borrow, and I have never given it back. What do you think?" I asked him gently, "Well, would you like my honest opinion?" He said, "Sure." I responded, "You look like a ten-year-old boy wearing his dad's suit." The shoulders were way too big, the arms almost reached his fingertips, and the pants were all sagging at the ankles. You see, Henry is five inches shorter than his friend Johnny.

I said to him: "There is no way you are wearing this suit as my date, so please take it off and give it back to Johnny. We are going to buy you a tailor-made suit." We got in the car immediately and drove to the store downtown. Henry had never spent more than fifty dollars on a piece of clothing and had never owned anything this expensive. He was measured and fitted, and the salesman found the perfect suit for him.

He put on a suit that was tailor-made for his size and shape. I wish you could have seen the look on his face as he felt the difference between what a tailored suit feels like compared to an ill-fitted, borrowed suit from a friend. He has never looked back since that day, and now he dresses with style because he understands the value of a well-made suit.

Now that we are in Christ, we are dressed in a new wardrobe. We no longer have to wear the ill-fitting rags of shame. Instead, our Master Tailor wants to fit us with a perfectly designed spiritual wardrobe that is just for us. Colossians 3:9–14 explains this process of taking off the filthy rags of Satan's lies and putting on the garment of God's truth:

> Don't lie to one another. You're done with that old life. It's like a filthy set of ill-fitting clothes you've stripped off and put in the fire. Now you're dressed in a new wardrobe. Every item of your new way of life is custom-made by the Creator, with his label on it. All the old fashions are now obsolete. Words like Jewish and non-Jewish, religious and irreligious, insider and outsider, uncivilized and uncouth, slave and free, mean nothing. From now on everyone is defined by Christ, everyone is included in Christ. So, chosen by God for this new life of love, dress in the wardrobe God picked out for you: compassion, kindness, humility, quiet strength, discipline. Be even-tempered, content with second place, quick to forgive an offense. Forgive as quickly and completely as the Master forgave you. And regardless of what else you put on, wear love. It's your basic, all-purpose garment. Never be without it. (MSG)

The Bible is very clear on what we should wear and what we shouldn't wear. Things like hate, envy, jealousy, boastfulness, insecurity, arrogance, self-pity, guilt, shame, rivalry, manipulation, control, pride, competitiveness, weakness—these are all labels that do not reflect our Designer. These negative labels are a result of how we see ourselves through the lens of our sinful nature.

Like any good designer, God showcases more than one outfit in His collection. He wants our wardrobe to be varied and plentiful. The Bible lists many things we are to clothe ourselves with. Here are just a few:

Jesus

Above all, we are to clothe ourselves with Jesus Christ. We should reflect His character and His attitudes in everything we think and say. Galatians 3:27–29 says: "For all of you who were baptized into Christ have clothed yourselves with Christ. There is neither Jew nor Gentile, neither slave nor free, nor is there male and female, for you are all one in Christ Jesus. If you belong to Christ, then you are Abraham's seed, and heirs according to the promise."

Splendor

We are also to put on a garment of splendor. *Oxford Living Dictionaries* defines *splendor* as "magnificent features or qualities."[1] Think about this: Your Master Tailor designed you with magnificent features and qualities! He didn't design you to hide in shame or pretend you are invisible to avoid conflict or rejection. You are the image bearer of God, and God designed you to reflect His splendor. So take off your rags of shame, and put on your garment of splendor! "Gird your sword on your side, you mighty one; clothe yourself with splendor and majesty. In your majesty ride forth victoriously in the cause of truth, humility and justice; let your right hand achieve awesome deeds" (Psalm 45:3–5).

Strength and Dignity

The woman in Proverbs 31 apparently understood her tailor-made design. She reflected her Master Tailor in everything she did, from her daily routine to taking care of her family. She understood that God was her Designer, and she reflected His strength and His dignity in the way she interacted with people every day. The writer of Proverbs described her like this: "She is clothed with strength and dignity; she can laugh at the days to come" (Proverbs 31:25).

The Power of the Holy Spirit

No spiritual wardrobe would be complete without the power of the Holy Spirit. Before He ascended into heaven, Jesus promised His disciples that He would send the Holy Spirit. When the Holy Spirit came, Jesus said, His followers would be "clothed with power": "I am going to send you what my Father has promised; but stay in the city until you have been clothed with power from on high" (Luke 24:49).

Humility

One of the most beautiful features of our tailor-made design is humility. Although we are sons and daughters of the King of kings, we are not to be filled with pride or act as if we are superior to anyone else. Instead, we are to reflect our Master Tailor's design of humility. "Clothe yourselves with humility toward one another, because, 'God opposes the proud but shows favor to the humble'" (1 Peter 5:5).

Righteousness

Another garment in our tailor-made wardrobe is righteousness. Righteousness simply means to be morally right. Righteous people are able to make morally right choices because they know God's Word and are led by the Holy Spirit. When we put on the garment of righteousness, we are supernaturally empowered to think and to act in ways that are pleasing to God, and we are able to recognize and reject Satan's lies that attempt to lead us down paths of destruction. "I put on righteousness as my clothing; justice was my robe and my turban" (Job 29:14).

Encouragement

Encouragement is a garment that not only reflects the character of our Master Tailor but also helps us share His beautiful design with others! When we adorn ourselves with the garment of encouragement, we are able to use our words to help others discover their own true identities. We teach and admonish them to learn how to live out their own tailor-made design. "Let the message of Christ dwell among you richly as you teach and admonish one another with all wisdom through psalms, hymns, and songs from the Spirit, singing to God with gratitude in your hearts. And whatever you do, whether in word or deed, do it all in the name of the

Lord Jesus, giving thanks to God the Father through him"
(Colossians 3:16–17).

Love

The Bible says that we should clothe ourselves with compassion, kindness, humility, gentleness, and patience. But the most important of all the virtues we are to adorn ourselves with is *love*. Love is the showstopper, the *pièce de résistance*. Love is the element that completes the look of the ensemble God wants us to wear. It's what ties it all together:

> As God's chosen people, holy and dearly loved, clothe yourselves with compassion, kindness, humility, gentleness and patience. Bear with each other and forgive one another if any of you has a grievance against someone. Forgive as the Lord forgave you. And over all these virtues put on love, which binds them all together in perfect unity.
> (Colossians 3:12–14)

God is love (1 John 4:8), which is why love is in the fabric of how we are made. When we choose to wear hate, we put on cheap, ill-fitted clothing. Hate is not true to the original design. The truth is that every person has been made in the image of God. When we are able to love ourselves, love people, and look beyond the labels they are wearing, we can see the truth that everyone is tailor-made by the same Designer and is wearing His label—the label of son or daughter of the King of kings. This is a priceless label, one to be revered and honored.

WHAT LABEL ARE YOU WEARING?

It's time to look closely and see what label God has placed over your life.

The Spirit of God *is* our label. He took the dust from the earth and formed it into His image. He designed and created us, and we are His workmanship, just as Louis Vuitton or Chanel created material objects that have great value because the designer's stamp or label is placed on them. Our label is written on our hearts, and we are priceless. You are a one-of-a-kind design, unable to be replicated or copied by another. You no longer have the right to see yourself as any less valuable than a priceless, unique work of art. This is our true label.

What false label have you been wearing for years that still traps you? Ask the Lord to rearrange those words into something that will empower you rather than discourage you.

Why don't you take a minute and ask the Lord what name He calls you? Then allow Him to replace the lie you have been answering to with the truth He says about you. Close your eyes and imagine that Jesus is standing in front of you, and pray this prayer:

Dear Lord,

I choose to hand back the name I have been answering to—the one that has been holding me captive for so long. I repent for believing the lie that this is who I am. Lord, please bring Your healing touch to the hurt in my heart. I ask You now to speak Your name over me. I choose to believe, accept, and receive what You think about me. Help me to see myself as You see me.

In Your name, amen.

CHAPTER SIX

INSECURITY IS NOT A GOOD LOOK ON ANYONE

Insecurity is a waste of time.
—Diane von Furstenberg[1]

I was a hot mess! I was terribly insecure in so many areas. I had zero self-confidence. I hated having my photo taken because I felt unattractive, always focusing on my imperfections. I continually compared myself to everyone around me.

Growing up, I had a tiny freckle on my face just left of my nose. It was cute when I was six, but as I continued to grow, so did this freckle. My mum would often look at me and say: "Isn't God so good that He gave you a beauty spot right on your face? Many actresses in the old Hollywood movies would have to place one on their faces with an eyeliner pencil, but you have been kissed by God with one." In my little heart, I loved this beauty spot. By the age of sixteen, this beauty spot had grown large and was very visible. It was the first thing you saw on my face. But my mum had spent the past ten years telling me that it was what made me beautiful. Even though I had low self-esteem, that one comment helped me believe I had some sort of beauty.

One day I was catching the bus from downtown to my home. I got on the bus like every other day, but that day something happened that shattered my heart and added to the shame I already felt about myself. The only feature I'd been told was beautiful turned ugly. That day I got on the bus, and it was full of people: mothers with babies, students on their way home from school, and elderly citizens who had made their way into the city. There were no empty seats, so I stood in the aisle of the bus, holding onto the steel pole to keep myself from falling every time the bus moved from each stop.

As I was standing there minding my own business and dreaming about what snack I was going to devour when I got home, a young boy looked up at me and pointed to my face. He cringed and said: "Ew! What is that ugly mole on her face? It's hideous!" I couldn't believe my ears. What did he mean? I was extremely embarrassed as everyone around me looked straight at my face. If the bus could have ejected me that day, I would have greatly appreciated it. I froze in embarrassment, not knowing what to say as his mother hushed him. I felt my face go bright red. I wanted to hide but couldn't. There I was, exposed to everyone looking at my face. Suddenly my beauty spot became an "ugly mole."

Because I was self-conscious and felt ugly, I began to pull others down. For some reason, criticizing others made me feel a little better about myself for a short while. I hated so much about myself that I was my worst critic. I am relieved I did not live in the world we live in now, in a time when social media has the power and influence to dictate how we feel about ourselves.

I was so riddled with insecurity and felt so ashamed of who I was that I remember walking into a room where my sister and her friends were staying one night after a youth group meeting. The teenagers were hanging out and eating pizza, as they did most weekends. I was the annoying little sister she so graciously had to bring along with her, because my mum had said so. I was eight years younger than my sister, and I felt like the odd one out because of my age. On this evening, everyone had a seat around a large dining table, and I was the only one without a chair. No one noticed that I was standing up, and no one seemed to care. I just stood there, not knowing what to do or how to make anyone aware that I needed something. I was paralyzed by the fear that if I asked for help, no one would respond. I stood there wishing I had the power to make myself invisible.

The negative thoughts in my head began to consume me. In my distorted self-perception, I honestly believed that people were deliberately trying to shame me and leave me out. My rejection was the lens I was looking through in this scenario. It caused me to process vain imaginations in my mind that were debilitating. My thoughts told me that everyone at the table was talking about me and discussing how stupid I looked standing up against the wall. I perceived that they were making fun of me and that they enjoyed watching how uncomfortable I was. The reality was, they probably didn't even notice I was there—not because they were being mean, but because they likely thought I *wanted* to stand there. I was the proverbial wallflower who wanted to hide because I felt everyone else would see right through me and dislike what they saw. Insecurity had shut me down to the point where I was unable to engage with another person.

We are not designed to live this way. God made us to be confident and secure in Him, so that out of that loving relationship, we could operate within the fullness of who we are and be a blessing to those around us.

THE CURE FOR INSECURITY

The dictionary defines *insecurity* as "not confident or sure; not adequately guarded or sustained; not firmly fastened or fixed; not highly stable or well-adjusted; beset by fear and anxiety."[2] Insecurity is multifaceted. Just look at the multiple definitions for this one word! When insecurity rears its ugly head, it can cause a wide array of issues.

When we are insecure, we often compare ourselves to others to see how we measure up. Insecurity causes us to be inward-focused instead of others-focused. Insecurity always asks, "How does this affect *me*?" and, "What about *me*?" Me, me, me, and more me. This kind of unhealthy self-focus thwarts God's plan for us. The Enemy wants us to keep looking at ourselves for comparison, highlighting what we don't have and all the ways we are different from one another. This takes the focus away from who God is and what He can do with us if we are secure in Him.

When we don't realize what is inside of us, we will not live up to that opportunity. It's like receiving a million-dollar check with your name on it, but instead of depositing it in your bank account, you place it on your refrigerator door— staring at it all day without claiming its contents. You can even tell people you are a millionaire, but you will not be living like one. Unless you deposit that check and start withdrawing from that account, you will not be living a millionaire's life. Too many of God's children live like paupers, when in truth we are royalty, according to Scripture. We have the King of kings and Lord of lords living inside of us. We carry His name and seal of ownership, yet most of us are still wondering whether we measure up to the person next to us.

A SHIFT OF PERSPECTIVE

Throughout the Bible, every battle and every strategy looks different. God never uses the same formula. God uses unconventional people and moves in mysterious ways. We serve a God who parts the Red Sea and allows a wall of fire to keep the enemy from advancing (Exodus 14). We serve a God who sends rain down in a drought and burns up a wet altar (1 Kings 18:16–39). We serve a God who can make the sound of an army seem real, when in fact it's actually a few lepers walking into a camp to take hold of the spoils (2 Kings 7:3–8). We serve a God who speaks a word and silences a storm (Matthew 8:23–27).

I believe there is wisdom in the counsel of many, but when it comes to God requiring you to step out in faith, He may need you to do what He says—nothing more or nothing less. Sometimes leaders can be well meaning with their advice, using their own experience, education, and biblical knowledge to guide you. But God might have a different strategy for you. This is why it's important to know the voice of the Father and the design He has tailor-made for you.

For years, I allowed someone else to be the voice of God for my life. I felt as if I couldn't hear the voice of God for myself. I was so fearful of making the wrong decision. Because I had been labeled "stupid" as a child, I chose to look for a tangible person to help make those decisions for me. I found a woman who became my mentor, but our relationship soon became unhealthy because my dependence transferred to her instead of to God. Her opinion began to dictate every part of my life, including what food I liked, how I dressed, and how I wore my hair. My opinion never measured up. I thought she always had better ideas, better products, and better clothes, which made me feel inferior. I found myself agreeing with things she liked even though I didn't like them at all. When she said something was cool, everyone said it was cool.

Before I knew it, I morphed into being just like her while losing my own identity, all because I did not think I was good enough, pretty enough, or smart enough compared to her. My family could see it clearly, but no one could talk to me about it. I thought I had found my security in a friendship with a mentor. She became the voice of reason in my life because I was looking for validation in all the wrong places. Little did I know I was still bound by the fear of what other people thought of me. After about thirteen years of living like this, everything came to a crescendo. I love how God does this because He is jealous for us (Exodus 34:14), and He does not want another person taking His place in our lives.

I wrote in my journal the details of one day of my life during this season of feeling incredibly insecure. Here is a sample:

Life has been rather difficult lately. God has been stretching my capacity and dealing with issues of my heart, especially in the area of my insecurities. It's amazing how in your own mind, the grass is always greener on the other side. I had imagined that life would finally start to unfold as I had always dreamed it would. I would be preaching and changing the world with the gift inside of me. I thought by now that Henry and I would finally be free to be who we are and fulfill the call on our lives together.

Today my thoughts have taken me in a destructive downward spiral. I am completely messed up on the inside. I feel sorry for myself, and I feel like I have never felt so alone and helpless. Feelings of rejection and isolation have set in, and I am falling down a dark hole. My internal dialogue goes something like this: My friends don't appreciate me anymore. They are hiding things from me because they don't want me around them right now. They are sick of me, and they don't like me. They are just pretending to like me. I want to run away. I can't live like this anymore.

At the time, I was viewing my current circumstances through a wounded, rejected, self-absorbed filter. Before I knew it, my negative thoughts and I were speaking to one another about how much my friends hated me and how no one really cared about me. It was all too difficult, and I just wanted to run a million miles away.

The irrational thoughts continued to spiral down—so much that I started to believe my life was a waste of time. Maybe I wasn't supposed to be here. After all, I was an accident that just happened to be born.

One day, I was feeling so insecure and down about myself that I screamed, I cried, and I wept bitterly about how bad my life was. After I had finished spewing my woes, I decided to take some time out for a little retail therapy. As I drove out to the shops, I sensed the small, still voice of the Holy Spirit saying, *Why don't you watch that DVD that was given to you of how great God is?* I thought in response: *Are you kidding me? Who can be bothered with watching a DVD about space?*

I felt the Lord say again, *You should watch that DVD.* The thought kept nagging me, so later that day, I reluctantly went into my lounge and watched it.

I began to listen to Louie Giglio, founder of Passion City Church, speak about how great our God is.[3] At first I felt as if I was sitting in a science class, and I wondered, *How is this going to help me?* But I knew that I had to keep watching until the end. As Louie continued to speak about the greatness of God, my perspective began to shift. I went from looking at my own pathetic circumstances to seeing how much more powerful my God was. I began to sob as I saw God in His glory and how detailed He was in creating everything on earth, including us. I knelt on the carpet and repented for allowing my circumstances and the voice of the Enemy to dictate my thinking, which had changed my behavior for the worse. How could I have become so limited and small-minded in my view of who He was?

Something Louie said struck a chord with me. He said that sin had caused us to shift our perspective to view God as limited and small, and to view ourselves as big and puffed up. Oh my goodness—that was me right then and there. When we stop letting God be God, we start trying to do for ourselves the things that He is meant to do for us.

Louie also said that our great God, in all His majesty and wonder, loves us so much that He will hold us in His hand and never let us go, no matter the circumstances. His purpose is not to change our circumstances but to change us amid the circumstances we are facing. In these moments, we need to consciously decide to take every thought captive and surrender it to Christ (2 Corinthians 10:5).

Our choices often determine how successful we will be in life. So many of us throw in the towel and walk away right before a breakthrough. Sometimes your greatest meltdown will be right before your greatest breakthrough. Choose to listen to the small, quiet voice of the Holy Spirit, because He knows you better than anyone else.

DISCOVERING OUR DESIGN

Increased dependence on God—having an active awareness of Him and a heightened sense to see and hear His heart—only comes when we are alone long enough to silence all other external voices. Sometimes He needs to bring us into a season where we are totally alone so that we will be forced to listen. You can throw a tantrum and miss out on what God wants to do, or you can choose to yield to the season you are in and allow God to reveal His mysteries to you.

You may be in a tough place in your life right now, but know that Jesus is holding you together in the midst of chaos. God will bring good out of all difficulties, troubles, suffering, and hardships (Romans 8:28). The best scenario to come out of your life is that you will better relate to and become more like Jesus. You will also be able to walk others through their breakthroughs, because even though the Enemy's design is to destroy you, Jesus turns around to decorate you with the names "overcomer" and "champion." The promise is limited to those who love God and have submitted to His way of doing things, so that He can work on your behalf and bring beauty out of ashes.

We are marked by God's majesty and are fashioned and formed in His image. You have been "fearfully and wonderfully made" (Psalm 139:14). You can hope in and wait on the Lord (Psalm 27:14). To those who stand right in the middle of chaos, pain, and adversity and determine not to run away, but to stand and believe God, here is your promise: "Those who hope in the LORD will renew their strength. They will soar on wings like eagles; they will run and not grow weary, they will walk and not be faint" (Isaiah 40:31).

Something inside me woke up that day after watching the DVD. I received healing in a place in my heart that I had not allowed anyone to visit. I realized if a God who is so big and powerful took the time to be so detailed in creating me, then I have no excuse to be anything but glorious for Him—for I was fearfully and wonderfully made in His image. I discovered that I was good enough as me. It was as if I became a new person, but I was actually just discovering myself—finally. I had thrown out all the junk that had piled on top of who I was born to be. The clutter had been in the way, burying who I was.

Piece by piece, Jesus removed the debris I had accumulated over the years. Every lie I believed about myself was lifted, and I discovered a pot of gold that had always been living inside of me buried deep down. I discovered that I was valuable. I discovered that I was creative and intelligent. I discovered that people loved being around me. I discovered that I had a unique sense of style. I finally saw that Alex was a good person. Everything started to change. I wore what I wanted. I ate what I wanted. I did what I liked for the first time in years, and I didn't care what anyone thought.

I began to allow God's voice to become the loudest voice in my heart. After many layers of healing, I had to go through the grieving process of all those years that felt wasted because of my insecurities. When I look back at photos of myself during that season, it's astounding to see the difference between then and now. I look older and so very sad in those old pictures. I now love who I am and know that I was born to leave a mark that no one else but me can leave.

I can't believe I used to feel so ugly; I can't believe I allowed those feelings to skew my ability to trust deeply because I was afraid that those who came close could potentially hurt me. Then I began to see myself how God sees me. I allowed God to heal my heart. By yielding to Him, I entered the process of being transformed into a beautiful daughter who found her security and identity in belonging to my heavenly Father, which has helped me rise above all insecurity and fear.

God has called each of us to do something great. He may

not have you do it in the same way He has called others to do it, but each one of us has been given a measure of grace (Ephesians 4:7). You are tailor-made to fulfill the destiny God has purposed for you. We each reflect a part of God's limitless DNA as individuals. So stay true to your tailor-made design and ask God to reveal to you His divine strategy for your life.

BEING FITTED ON THE INSIDE

Our biggest battles are sometimes the everyday things we have to deal with, such as insecurity. When God is working on the inside of us, He is patient through the process. When a tailor is fitting a suit, those fittings take time—and the designer pays close attention to the details. In a much bigger way, God takes into consideration where you will grow up, who you will be in contact with, what your gifting is, and what circumstances you will encounter as He fashions you for your destiny. Even if your life experiences have been tragic or negative, He will make the necessary alterations so that the result of His design is beautiful and without blemish. You will become a truly beautiful, tailor-made garment.

> *Dear Lord,*
>
> *I repent of struggling with feelings of insecurity and needing validation from people. I choose to receive my identity in You. I want to know who I am in Christ, and I know You don't make mistakes. I choose to find my security in You and pray that I would live from a whole and healed heart.*
>
> *In Your name, amen.*

CHAPTER SEVEN

WHO IS MY FATHER?

"For as he thinks in his heart, so is he."
Proverbs 23:7 (NKJV)

My kids loved it when we read them P. D. Eastman's classic book *Are You My Mother?*[1] It's the story of a baby bird that hatches while his mother is away looking for food. He goes on a desperate search to find her, and along the way he asks questions of all the wrong animals and objects. He goes to a kitten, a dog, a hen, a cow, a boat, a plane. Lastly, he climbs onto a bulldozer, asking them all if they are his mother. When they all say no, the little bird cries out in desperation. He knows he has a mother, but he doesn't know what she looks like. The story ends with the bulldozer dropping the baby bird back in its nest and his mother arriving shortly thereafter with food. The baby bird's mother asks him, "Do you know who I am?" The baby bird suddenly realizes that *this* is his mother! His mother is not a kitten or a dog or any of those other creatures because his mother is the one who looks like him, who came looking for him, and who brought provision for him.

Like this baby bird, we may be on a quest to find out who we belong to. Some of us don't know who our real mother and father are, while others—like me—know who their parents are but sometimes wish they were from another family. Growing up, I always felt like a square peg in a round hole, wondering how on earth I came from my family because I felt like the odd one out. I began to look in other places to try and find a sense of belonging. Friends became an escape. I preferred to be at other people's homes. I lived vicariously through characters in movies, and that became my escape mechanism. Teachers became the source of my validation. Yet nothing ever hit the spot of making me feel that I belonged.

Maybe we are looking in all the wrong places as we try to discover who we belong to. In the meantime, God has been pursuing us and directing our steps to get us to a place where we come face-to-face with Him. There He will ask us, "Do you know who I am?"

All of us are curious to know why we look and behave the way we do. This explains why, when children discover that they are adopted, they often feel something is missing until they find out who their biological parents are. Until they learn the identity of their birth parents, questions plague their minds: *Who do I resemble? Who do I share my personality type with? What does my history look like? How do I fit in if I don't know who I'm connected to?* There is something in all of us that wants to feel connected to someone, to know that we belong. Part of knowing who we are is knowing where we come from. This gives us an innate sense of security and identity.

I struggled with my identity because I bought into the false idea that my parents were the reason I am here. Therefore, I placed my significance in who my parents were and who they were not. You may have been planned by your parents or unplanned—but it doesn't matter, because God had already designed His perfect plan for you long before your parents were even born. Therefore, we need to get to know the source of our beginning. The only One who knows the "why" into which we were born is God the Father.

THERE ARE NO UNPLANNED CHILDREN

According to God's Word, there is no such thing as an unplanned child. Psalm 139:16 says, "Your eyes saw my unformed body; all the days ordained for me were written in your book before one of them came to be." Jeremiah 1:5 says, "Before I formed you in the womb I knew you, before you were born I set you apart." As I pondered on those verses for a while, I began to think about the many stories in the Bible of great men and women of God who were born as a product of adultery, incest, or a night spent with a prostitute. Others were adopted and cared for by strangers. Solomon, who became king of Israel, was born out of adultery. Moses was adopted by Pharaoh's daughter, was raised to be a prince, and then became the deliverer of Israel. Jephthah was born from a night spent with a prostitute and grew up a rebel, but then he became a victorious warrior who led Israel into a mighty victory. Perez was born out of incest, yet God placed him in the lineage of Christ through the line of King David, the tribe of Judah. These illegitimate children went on to become some of the most influential people ever written about.

Even Jesus was considered illegitimate by many who couldn't comprehend His being conceived by the Holy Spirit. Unfathomable! It seems impossible, but God's ways are always higher than ours. God chose to come to earth as a baby, and He used Mary's womb as the vessel to enter our world. Jesus did not arrive like Arnold Schwarzenegger in *Terminator*, who came out of nowhere as a fully developed man landing naked on the concrete in a back alley. Rather, Jesus chose to enter the world in a humble manner, as a seed that grew inside a young girl's womb.

God planned you before the creation of the world (Ephesians 1:4), and He had you in mind "for such a time as this" to reveal the glory of God on earth (Esther 4:14). Therefore, the womb in which we grew and the circumstances in which we were conceived have no bearing on our destiny. Whether your parents wanted you or not, God chose you and had a purpose in mind for you before the foundations of the world.

The Enemy has been lying to us for too long, deceiving us into believing we are insignificant and unworthy. He has spoken lies that say it matters who our parents are or what school we went to or what our financial status is—but none of those things holds any weight regarding your potential or how God sees you. According to Psalm 139, God sees you. He saw your unformed body, and He knit you together in your mother's womb. Every fiber of your being was designed by Him. The most important part of you—the part that makes you unique—is the spirit God put inside you. It's your spirit that makes you who you are. God designed you from the inside out, and He gave you your spirit, which you will take with you into eternity.

Our heavenly Father reveals to us who He is and who we are in Genesis 1:26–27:

> Then God said, "Let us make mankind in our image, in our likeness, so that they may rule over the fish in the sea and the birds in the sky, over the livestock and all the wild animals, and over all the creatures that move along the ground." So God created mankind in his own image, in the image of God he created them; male and female he created them.

We look like God and act like Him. The more we know Him and spend time with Him, the more we discover who we are and what we are truly capable of.

WE ARE THE SPITTING IMAGE OF OUR FATHER

The phrase *spitting image* never made sense to me. Growing up with my parents, whose Italian accent and broken English provided much comedy during our childhood years, contributed to my habit of saying words incorrectly. As I grew older, I continued to misuse many of the phrases and sayings I heard as a child, which sent my husband into hysterical laughing fits many nights.

Spitting image was one of those expressions I always got wrong. I would say "splitting image" because my understanding of the phrase was that if you split two pictures in half of each person and put them next to each other, then it would be exactly the same. Makes sense, right? Of course not! It's rather ridiculous. But I was confident each time I uttered that phrase—that is, until my husband heard me and said, "Honey, the phrase is *spitting image*." I was so adamant I was right that I did what every person in the twenty-first century does: I Googled it. To my amazement and sheer horror, he was correct. As I looked at the definition a little closer, however, I learned that *spitting image* means "a person who bears a strong physical resemblance to another, especially to a relative."[2] I love that definition because it couldn't be truer regarding who we are. We are the spitting image of our heavenly Father because we were made in His likeness; therefore, we carry His image and have attributes like our Father. Because sin has distorted our view of who God is, it has also distorted the way we see ourselves. God gave us His Word to show us His character and nature. That is where we must look to learn about Him. Only then will we begin to understand His likeness and ours.

At creation, God tailor-made us all with specific attributes, which are revealed and displayed throughout our lives when we understand who we are in Him. As we renew our minds by developing a personal relationship with our heavenly Father, the Bible says we are being conformed to His likeness, in Christ's image (Romans 8:29; 12:2). Therefore, *you* become the spitting image of God!

If you are struggling with low self-esteem, then there is a disconnect between how you see yourself and who you really are. It's time to start seeing yourself through the lens of who God says you are, not through the lens of where you have come from, who your biological parents are, or what others may have negatively spoken over you.

THE FILTER I VIEWED GOD THE FATHER THROUGH

Unfortunately, many of us view ourselves in a negative way because of our fallen nature, or we view God through the dysfunctional filter of our earthly parents. Thus, we perceive God by comparing our earthly parents against Him. My view of God was certainly skewed growing up, because I viewed God the Father through the filter of my relationship with my earthly father.

I blamed most of my issues growing up on my parents. I would often say to myself: *If I had been born into a different family, I would not be this way. Maybe if I had a family that could speak English fluently, I would do better in school. Maybe if I had been born into a family that lived like the* Brady Bunch, *I would be more secure in who I am. If only we had stayed in Italy, then I would fit in more with the other Italians and wouldn't have to fit in with the Australians around me. If only our family didn't have so many problems. . . .* The list went on. We could all come up with every excuse in the world for the way we are—and believe me, I had plenty of blame to dish out.

Don't misunderstand me; I loved my dad so much. He

was a sweet and kind father to us. He was quiet, but he could also be funny, and he worked hard to provide for his family. He had been brought up on a farm in Italy, which called for hard manual labor. He did not enjoy farm life, so he decided to migrate to Australia. He was an old soul, even at nineteen, which made him an extremely responsible young man. At home, he had been one of ten children and got lost in the crowd. Coming to Australia was his chance to stand out and make something of himself.

He was very melancholy in nature, a deep thinker who processed everything internally, which meant he would retreat for days without speaking to anyone. At the age of twenty-eight, he married my mother, who was a fireball, to say the least. "Full of pepper," as she likes to describe herself. She was loud and opinionated, while Dad was a man of few but extremely wise words. Needless to say, they often clashed. My mother married my father out of convenience and was not in love with him. Can you imagine what that did to his self-esteem? From the outset, our home had several holes in the fabric.

As a young girl, I longed to hear my father say, "I love you," "You are beautiful," and, "You are my princess." But those words hardly ever came. I know he thought those things about me, but because he was an internal processor he kept most of it buried inside. My father had a bruised heart. But since I was a little girl who did not understand the complexities of a broken heart, all I saw was a dad who was present in my home yet absent in affirming me with his words. I looked to him for affirmation and affection, yet I felt there was always something missing. He may have been there physically, but he was hardly ever involved in my life.

My father's language of love was provision. So as far as he was concerned, he showed us that he adored us by working so hard and never letting us go without. In his mind, by providing for us he was displaying love at its highest capacity.

But I had a different love language. Even though he was a good provider, all I wanted was for my dad to spend time with me and tell me that I was his precious little girl. I needed to hear affirming words from him. I wanted so badly to be validated by him. I needed his voice to be the one shaping how I saw myself at an early age.

In life, the circumstances we experience, whether good or bad, shape the way we view things. When things go wrong consistently, our view can look bleak and hopeless. It may feel as if there is no light at the end of the tunnel and that God is not paying attention to what is going on. When these circumstances reach a boiling point, we tend to view everything through a critical, negative, and fearful filter. We get annoyed at the slightest things, we begin to anticipate that everything that can go wrong will go wrong, and we start to declare those negative things over our life before anything has actually happens—all because we are looking through a dirty filter.

When this happens, we need to pause for a moment and realize that maybe things aren't as bad as they seem. Instead, maybe the problem is the filter we are looking through. When we have a faulty filter, no matter what comes our way, we automatically perceive it as negative. How you perceive something eventually becomes your truth. I have observed three siblings grow up in the same household with the same parents and the same upbringing, yet if I were to ask all three about their perspective on a scenario, each one would say something different because of the individual filters they see things through.

So many of us view God through a filter of how our fathers treated us. I never had a problem seeing God the Father as a provider, but I did have trouble seeing God as someone who wanted a personal relationship with me. Did He see me as beautiful, or did He even see me at all? I never felt beautiful, because those words of affirmation didn't come easily for my father. He didn't seem interested in the things I was interested in, such as singing, acting, and fashion. So when it came to my desires and dreams, I thought God was too busy to care. Why would He bother with such small details when He had the world to run?

Because my father was a man of few words, he rarely affirmed my abilities and talents. Even though he was proud of me, his absence from my performances and school events sent a message to me that he wasn't interested in my extracurricular activities. All I wanted was for my dad to watch and then tell me he was proud of me. He was always so tired after a hard day's work, but I took that to mean he didn't think what I was doing was important. I began to look for affirmation from other people, such as friends and schoolteachers. Later in my young adult life, I looked for that affirmation from people in church leadership.

LOOKING IN ALL THE WRONG PLACES

Just like the baby bird who looked for his mother, I was looking in all the wrong places to find validation and acceptance.

In the meantime, God the Father had been whispering to my heart, *Do you know who I am?* I did not recognize Him because I was looking for someone tangible, someone I could physically feel and audibly hear. God seemed too distant and far too busy to be concerned with the details of my life. Therefore, I kept roaming around until I found something—anything, good or bad—to make me feel that I was loved.

I remember being so desperate to be loved that when the first boy asked me to be his girlfriend, I jumped into a relationship with my whole heart, even though I was fractured and broken. I truly believed this boy was the missing piece that would fill the gaping hole inside my heart. For three years, I was determined to make this relationship work, even though my parents did not approve of him. I hid the relationship from them and in defiance was going to prove to my parents that this boy was the answer to my freedom. But the truth was, he and I were both fractured and broken from parent issues, and we were trying to get from each other what only God the Father could give. Even though we did have moments of happiness and fun times, in my heart I knew this relationship was not the answer for my life. The boy had no interest in serving God or going to church, and I think he blamed God for what had happened in his own family. He had major trust issues.

Our relationship got to the point where every time I was with him I felt love and acceptance, but the moment I drove home I felt empty and aimless. We would go out and drink—and he would drink excessively, which broke my heart. One night I had a moment when I knew God was calling me to a relationship with Him. As I stood at the bar, it felt as if my world went into slow motion. I looked around me at all the aimless people in the club. They were dancing, but as I saw them in slow motion, they looked vacant and sad. They were trying to get a high that would make them feel alive, yet all I saw was emptiness and aimlessness.

At that moment, I sensed the voice of God in my heart, saying: *I have called you to live a life that is better than this. I have a purpose for you that is exciting and full of the love you are searching for. This is not your destiny.* I got up from that moment, called a taxi, and went straight home. When I got into my bedroom, I cried out to God and said: "This is not working. I am not happy. If You are who You say You are, then come and change my life!" At that moment I decided to draw a line in the sand (which was actually my carpet) and cross over to a life with Jesus as my Lord. I gave my heart afresh to God—not a portion of my heart, not 99 percent of my heart, but my whole heart. I had been looking in all the wrong places to find peace and love and belonging, and I chose to give it all to Jesus that night.

The first thing I felt Jesus say to give Him was my boyfriend of three years. This was a hard thing to do because I was emotionally dependent on him, but I knew for this new life to work, I had to give Jesus everything. I gave Him my relationship and decided to pursue Jesus relentlessly instead of pursuing the wrong people, hoping to find acceptance and validation.

Unfortunately, instead of finding my acceptance in this new relationship with Jesus, I replaced my boyfriend with other people. Church leaders became parental figures for me. I attended a large church that had incredible leaders. In this church, I was baptized and encountered God in a tangible way. In my mind, the pastors of the church were the closest thing to Jesus. I thought they could do no wrong, that they had arrived at a standard of holiness that I was years away from achieving.

I had built a false image in my mind about these church leaders. I thought they were better than me and my family. They knew the Word of God better than I did, and if the Bible were still being written, I would have seen them as the patriarchs. I wished I had been born into a family like theirs, because from a distance their family looked perfect. All my friends were pastors' kids. Because I was the only girl in our church group who wasn't a pastor's kid, I felt inferior to them. They never would have guessed that, though, because I was the life of the party and the easygoing girlfriend who always went with the flow.

As I got older, I found myself serving the church leadership like a slave. Whenever they called, I dropped everything to serve them. Whatever they needed, I made sure I provided. If they gave me instructions on how to live, I obeyed. I developed an unhealthy codependency on them. I subconsciously became part of their family because in my mind their family was perfect. I developed an approval addiction from them. I gave them authority to speak into my life, and before I knew it, I was a devoted follower, neglecting my own family in the process.

I thought this family at church would fulfill my sense of belonging and become the security I thought I was looking for. The problem is, when we divert our devotion to another human being, we fall short because our fractured hearts long for the true love and acceptance that only comes from God. Because I was broken from my own family, I viewed any authority in my life through a filter of rejection. So when affirmation didn't come from my church leaders, my world began to pull apart at the seams. I would try harder to do better. I would exhaust myself in pleasing them. I would buy them gifts and serve their vision just so I could receive validation. Of course, at the time this was happening, I thought I was serving the local church—but now that I am older, wiser, and free, I can see that I was striving to belong and have someone validate me. At the time, I didn't feel validated by anyone. Even though I had a relationship with Jesus, I still didn't fully understand who I was or what it was that I was supposed to do with my life.

We all look to something to fill the void that only Jesus can fill. For some of us it's alcohol, drugs, food, and relationships. For others it's a career or money and material possessions. To change our hearts, we need to change how we view things. We need God to clean our hearts from the inside out, which will wipe away the debris so we can begin to perceive things clearly rather than through a murky, smudged filter.

IN CONSTANT PURSUIT

The need for a loving and involved father on earth is completely valid. You only need to go to a playground and listen to all the children calling out to their dads, saying, "Look at me, Dad!" "Dad, watch me go down the slide." Or watch the child who is in the school play. Even though there are hundreds in the auditorium, all she wants to see is her dad's face. Dads are heroes. We think they can do anything.

When I was young, if a storm was brewing outside and my dad was home, I would run into his arms and snuggle in. I felt a sense of safety and security, thinking, *If Dad is here, then all is right with the world.* Unfortunately, not all fathers have been present in their children's lives, which has triggered insecurity and caused dysfunction.

Our earthly fathers can warp our perspective of God in many ways. You need only look at the effects of a fatherless generation to see how broken families can become. A father helps shape our sense of identity, security, protection, and provision. If any of these qualities has been broken, then we can subconsciously view our heavenly Father in the same way. An emotionally absent father can lead, as it did with me, to difficulty in connecting with God for fear that the moment you do give Him your heart, He will lose interest. An abusive father can leave you feeling unprotected, thus making God seem unsafe to trust. As our issues continue to pile up, we build self-protective mechanisms to compensate for what we never received in our families.

Inside every human being, God tailor-made a God-shaped hole that only He can fill. But He is a gentle Father who does not force a relationship with us because He also designed us with the free will to choose Him. He did not design us to be robots, since there is no satisfaction in having a relationship that is forced. It's vital that we take time to discover who our heavenly Father is.

God is unlike any father on earth. Whether you had the best father or the worst, God defies comparison because He is not human (Numbers 23:19). He cannot lie (Titus 1:2). He does not disappoint (Romans 5:5). He is good all the time, even when it feels as though He isn't. He has given us a love letter, the Bible, to show us His heart. The Bible is not a history book of facts about God; it is a book that is alive and active and sharper than any two-edged sword (Hebrews 4:12). God's Word has the power to transform our hearts and minds and teach us who He is—and who we are in Him.

If we don't have a true understanding of who God is as our Father, then we will constantly be trying to fill that hole with things that will never bring true security. If you never had your father's approval or affection, and you don't grasp how deeply God loves and approves of you, then you will often look for that missing approval and affection in others— usually in an unhealthy way. I know from personal experience that nothing compares to the genuine love from our Father God. Once you have experienced that love, you can't go back to anything else.

God the Father has been pursuing us even when we have not realized it. When we stop, take notice, and allow ourselves to answer His question—*Do you know who I am?*—we will finally discover who we really are. No one else knows us better than the Master Tailor who designed us from the inside out. Why don't you take a step toward Him and allow yourself to know Him better? The more you see Him and the more you get to know Him, the more you will become like Him and discover where you belong.

Dear Father,

I repent of trying to find acceptance from everyone else but You. I realize You are the source of my identity and I can only find true love in You. I choose to believe that You are my Father and that You love me with a relentless love. I ask You to come into my life and reveal who You are to me. I want You to be the source of my freedom. I surrender all the props that have been a counterfeit to Your real love, and I ask You to help me place my security in You. Thank You for loving me unconditionally.

In Jesus' name, amen.

CHAPTER EIGHT

FORGIVENESS
UNLOCKS FREEDOM

"Resentment is like taking poison and waiting for the other person to die."
—Malachy McCourt[1]

I threw my fist up at God, feeling hurt and abandoned that He was not answering my prayers the moment I prayed them. Why had God allowed my mum to be so angry? Why hadn't He changed her? As an adult, I was still facing the same issues with her that I did as a young girl. Even though I loved my mother because she was my mum, a part of my heart was so broken because of her words and actions that sometimes I couldn't stand her. I privately wrestled with hate and love on so many occasions and felt terrible that I felt this way, but I couldn't control my feelings. Certain buttons my mum would press sent me into an emotional downward spiral. I was waiting for the day she would change and realize her wrongs against me. I imagined this happening, and then we could finally have the wonderful relationship I had been longing for—a relationship without fear of being told I was wrong and stupid all the time. A relationship that went two ways. An exchange of unconditional love. But because she never changed, I felt the situation was hopeless.

One day I was reading Matthew 6:15 when these words jumped off the page at me: "If you do not forgive others their sins, your Father will not forgive your sins." It was as if a knife went through my heart. I realized, *I have unforgiveness in my heart against my mum.*

As I meditated on this verse, I discovered I had a deep root of unforgiveness toward my mother. I had buried the hurt and resentment from my childhood years. It was as if God began to play the movie reel of my life, and I saw right before my eyes all the times that I had vowed to never forgive her when she lashed out and hurt me. I remembered the pain of the cutting words she carelessly used to attack me in moments of frustration, her lack of nurture when I needed encouragement, and her overly harsh discipline. Even though I covered it up and pretended that it didn't affect me, I remained broken on the inside and full of resentment. I had locked away those memories in a place that no one was allowed to enter. Not even Jesus.

I was embarrassed that my family was fractured, so I never talked to anyone about it. After all, I grew up in church, and my mum was very involved there. Every time she would speak about the things of God, I felt as if a volcano was erupting inside me. I couldn't hear any words of wisdom that came out of her mouth because they sounded entirely hypocritical. She would preach and teach and give pearls of wisdom, yet I didn't respect any of it because I had buried hatred in my heart toward her.

I loved and honored her as my mother, but what I truly felt was resentment and anger. I justified my resentment because of the rejection I felt from her. I often thought: *She should know better. She is my mother and a Christian! Why is she being so cruel to me?* Because my house was a constant reminder of my turbulent childhood, I thought it would be best to move out and attempt to erase the past by not having to face it daily. How many of us run away to escape our fears and issues in hopes that they will just disappear? We can move to a new location, but we bring the same hurt and resentment with us wherever we go. Sooner or later, it will all come to the surface and demand to be dealt with once again.

I felt the Lord tell me that I should not move out of my home until I forgave my mother for what happened. I wrestled with this idea for some time and even tried to justify the reasons why it would be best for me to leave. But deep down, I knew I had to face this issue head-on if I were to be a successful doer of the Word, not just a hearer of the Word (James 1:22–25). It took a long time for me to truly forgive and release my mum from my resentment. I pleaded during many prayer times to receive healing, but a part of me still wanted my mum to pay for the hurt she had caused me. I thought that if I just forgave her, then she would get off the hook without paying for her actions. I didn't understand that I was drinking the poison I thought was meant for her. The poison of unforgiveness was killing me.

JESUS: A PICTURE OF FORGIVENESS

As I sat in my bedroom weeping, replaying my life in my mind and justifying my feelings of hurt and rejection, Jesus gave me a picture of Himself. He stood in front of Pilate and the crowd as an innocent man who had only come to do good and bring healing to a dying world. Only a week earlier the people had been singing, "Hosanna in the highest heaven!" (Matthew 21:9). And this week they were screaming, "Crucify him!" (Matthew 27:22). Yet He uttered not one word in His defense (Matthew 27:14). I can imagine Jesus looking over the crowd and seeing those He had healed and delivered. I can imagine Him feeling hurt by the people He had come to love and to heal, watching them stand with cold expressions, hating and mocking Him.

If that wasn't enough torture, they beat Jesus until He was unrecognizable. They handed Him over to be judged and hung on a cross. When He looked down from the cross—bleeding, bruised, and broken for us—He said these words that pierced my heart: "Father, forgive them, for they do not know what they are doing" (Luke 23:34). Instead of justifying Himself and asking the Father to punish the people who were hurting Him, Jesus took upon Himself their penalty of sin, shame, and death. He did this so those very same people would be able to receive forgiveness and atonement for their sin.

As I sat in my bed, meditating on the Word, Jesus's reaction unraveled me. I realized that I have no right to hold any resentment and unforgiveness toward anyone, let alone my own mother. God showed me that she loved me. She gave the best she knew how to give, but it was broken. I realized that my freedom was in my forgiveness toward her. I had been waiting for her to ask me for forgiveness, and because that never came, I was stuck in my pain—unable to move forward in true freedom.

So, with tears running down my face, overwhelmed by what Jesus had done for me, I finally yielded my rights and my justifications and my reasons for being upset. Then I handed them over to the One who understood my pain and suffering. I realized at that moment what true forgiveness really is. I understood how much God forgave us even when we were so undeserving. We who were destined for eternity without Him—for the wages of sin is death—received the gift of Himself, which is eternal life (Romans 6:23).

At that moment, I met the real Jesus. The Jesus who had mercy on me. The Jesus who looked at my filth and took my place in death so that I could live. At that moment I no longer needed my mother to say she was sorry. I chose to forgive her, no matter what.

That day I received my freedom, which has caused me to soar above the hurt and pain of the past. God used what the Enemy had meant to destroy me, and instead He sewed forgiveness into the fabric of my character, which in turn gave me hope to believe in a restored relationship with my mum. Stitch by stitch, the process of forgiveness brought beauty from my weathered garment.

I discovered the secret to my freedom was in forgiveness. This wasn't just a one-time moment, but I have gone to this place often to keep forgiving her—just like the Bible says, seventy-seven times (Matthew 18:22). Each time got easier and easier, and I discovered that when you have received supernatural love from God, the love you have for others also becomes supernatural. You don't have to try to love someone; you supernaturally love them with the love of Christ.

When we live from a place of abundant love, that's when "love covers over a multitude of sins" (1 Peter 4:8). This is the posture Jesus is talking about when He asks us to love our enemies and do good to those who hate us (Luke 6:27). It seems impossible, but when you realize how much you do not deserve God's mercy and forgiveness, you soon understand that, if you are in Christ Jesus, you have no right to hold unforgiveness toward anyone.

HEALING TAKES TIME

All of us were born with flaws. The Bible calls these flaws sin. Romans 3:23 says, "For all have sinned and fall short of the glory of God." Sin distorts God's original design, causing us to feel as though we don't fit. Sin also distorts our vision of God. In order to bring us back to our original design, the Master Tailor needs to make alterations so He can achieve a perfect fit. This process begins when we invite Jesus Christ as Savior and Lord into our hearts.

When Jesus comes in, He immediately washes away our sin. This is called justification. Isaiah 1:18 says, "Though your sins are like scarlet, they shall be as white as snow; though they are red as crimson, they shall be like wool." Jesus removes all the stains and blemishes from our heart. They are gone completely. The Bible says in Psalm 103:12, "As far as the east is from the west, so far has he removed our transgressions from us." It's important for us to understand that because Jesus died for our sins, we are now a new creation. Second Corinthians 5:17 says, "Therefore, if anyone is in Christ, the new creation has come: The old has gone, the new is here!"

We must allow God to cleanse our hearts, and we must accept by faith that we have a new start. In Christ, we are unblemished and beautiful. Even though our sin is completely gone, our minds need to be renewed. We need to learn how to bring our sinful nature into submission to the lordship of Christ. We may think becoming a Christian automatically sets us free. While this is true regarding our sin, we also need to work out our freedom through the renewal of our minds. We need to allow the process of sanctification to take place in our lives.

Romans 12:2 says: "Do not conform to the pattern of this world, but be transformed by the renewing of your mind. Then you will be able to test and approve what God's will is—his good, pleasing and perfect will." Renewing our minds requires two processes—justification and sanctification.

Justification means "to set something right, or to declare righteous."[2] We cannot do that on our own. Only by Jesus' shed blood were we made righteous in God's eyes. The Bible tells us there is no forgiveness for sins without the shedding of blood (Hebrews 9:22). In the Old Testament, people would sacrifice an animal to atone for their sins. In the New Testament,

God sent His only Son, who was without sin, to be the sacrificial lamb to die in our place and take the punishment we deserved. This sacrificial act allowed Christ's righteousness to be credited to us when we believe in Him (2 Corinthians 5:21).

Sanctification means to make something (or someone) holy. Here is a more official definition:

> The generic meaning of sanctification is "the state of proper functioning." To sanctify someone or something is to set that person or thing apart for the use intended by its designer. A pen is 'sanctified' when used to write. Eyeglasses are 'sanctified' when used to improve sight. In the theological sense, things are sanctified when they are used for the purpose God intends. A human being is sanctified, therefore, when he or she lives according to God's design and purpose.[3]

The process of sanctification is like altering a garment. Alterations take time. The results however, are always worth the delay. Because we live in an instant-gratification world where we can usually get what we want when we want it, having to wait on the sanctification process can be frustrating.

God is very interested in developing character in us. Our character is developed over time and fashioned by the choices we make. Trial and adversity are effective producers of character. They draw out what is inside us. We can allow the trials of life to consume us, or we can choose to overcome them. The Bible also promises us that sufferings can produce many godly qualities and become a source of hope for us. Romans 5:3–4 says, "Not only so, but we also glory in our sufferings, because we know that suffering produces perseverance; perseverance, character; and character, hope." The good news is that God's refining process does not end at strength of character, but instead with hope.

No one is immune from life's adversities, but we can all learn from our experiences. I am not saying that God delivers adversity to us, but He does use it to fashion and mold us into who we are meant to be. This is God's alteration process. He can work even our trials and tribulations into something beautiful. Enduring the process can sometimes be painful, but the gold it produces makes it more than worthwhile in the end.

If we look at the Word of God, we will see that the entire book tells a story of redemption taking place through the ages. The process *is* the destination—because as we are being altered, and the more alterations that are made, the more we are becoming like Jesus. Our ultimate goal should be to know Jesus and to be like Him. As followers of Christ, we need to stop complaining about how horrible the *process* is and start understanding that the process is necessary for our lives to be a perfect fit. We are going from glory to ever-increasing glory (2 Corinthians 3:18).

Most of us have struggled or are struggling with unforgiveness toward someone who has hurt us, abused us, or neglected us. Every time that person's name is mentioned, you may become filled with anxious thoughts. You may be waiting for that person to come to you and say they are sorry—but that day may never come. If you give your pain to the forgiving One who understands what it is like to be rejected and beaten and bruised, He will be faithful to heal your heart.

When you yield your offenses and hurts to Jesus, He will fill you with a love that overwhelms you and helps you see your situation from His perspective.

This is the secret to freedom. I discovered this freedom when I chose to forgive. I had to take responsibility for how I responded. It was my choice whether to hold onto bitterness or choose to forgive. God is a just God, and He is the One who vindicates and justifies us. When we place those who have hurt us in His hands, we allow Him the power to work on our behalf and to take that which was broken and turn it into a beautiful, redemptive testimony. You may never hear an apology from the people who hurt you, but it won't matter because you can receive the greatest gift from Jesus. His redemption far outweighs the need to hear those words.

Why don't you close your eyes and picture Jesus right now? Ask Him to show you the places you have kept hidden for so long. Ask Him to take you to that person in your mind's eye. Then look that person in the eye and say: "I choose to forgive you for [list those things that have hurt you]. I choose to cancel the debt you owe me. I release you from my judgment. I choose to forgive myself for the negative ways I responded to these hurts. In Jesus' name, amen."

Now, take a moment to allow the love of Jesus to wash over you and to heal those wounded parts that have been hidden for such a long time.

Dear Lord,

Today, I choose to release the person who has hurt me. I choose to forgive that person and to cancel the debt owed to me. Please help me be free of the hurt and negative consequences I experienced as a result of this person's words and actions. I choose to release all my hurts and offenses to You. Fill me with Your love, and help me see my situation from Your perspective.

In Your name, amen.

CHAPTER NINE

THE PROCESS IS
THE DESTINATION

He who began a good work in you will carry it
on to completion until the day of Christ Jesus.
—Philippians 1:6

I felt the call of God to full-time ministry when I was eleven years old. Even as a child, I had a burning desire to serve God. At one point, I wanted to become a nun like Mother Teresa. There was something about dedicating my life to Christ that felt right.

After ten years of growing up and finishing school, I started my first year at Bible college. I imagined that as soon as I completed my studies, I would be contacted by at least five churches that wanted me to begin serving their congregations in full-time ministry. Once I received that piece of paper certifying that I was qualified, then I would be ready to take on the world!

One day, I was sitting in a class listening to my lecturer, an older man who had shepherded the largest church in Australia at the time and had been faithfully serving the Lord for decades. Everyone looked up to him because he was an incredible visionary and minister. He opened his first lecture with this statement: "I have discovered over the years that God always takes us through an apprenticeship season of about ten years before we walk the destiny He has for us." I remember thinking: *Well, that is for the others in this room. It certainly doesn't apply to me.* After all, I received the call of God when I was eleven. I was then twenty-one, which I thought meant that I had already completed my ten years of apprenticeship. Oh, how wrong I was. I believed I was going to travel the world and confound the wise with my brilliant revelations. Ha! I cringe now, thinking about how arrogant I was back then. What was I thinking? I had nothing to say at twenty-one.

I achieved many accolades throughout the first year of my Christian studies. I was appointed as one of the class leaders, and I won the medal for being the all-around achiever in Bible college. I thought I was sure to be anointed and appointed of God after that! I thought: *Look at me, God. Look at how clever I am.* I thought I was attending Bible college to get schooled on theology, yet little did I know that God was beginning the work that needed to be done in my heart. He began dealing with a number of issues in my personal life that were quite painful—the first being my family.

Sometimes we think we are going into something to learn one thing, but God uses it to teach us what really matters. Even though God has given us a purpose and predestined us to do good works (Ephesians 2:10), He is far more interested in who we are than what we do. We focus so much on our plans that we try to fast-track the process of becoming like Him. But God wants our hearts before He wants our service. We need to discover our true identity in Christ before we do anything for Christ, because then we won't need what we do for Him to define who we are. I see too many people attempting to find their identity in what they do while neglecting who they are. God, in His kindness, uses the process to make us better from the inside out.

THE DRAGONFLY: A SYMBOL OF CHANGE

You may have asked yourself, *Why is there a picture of a dragonfly on the cover of this book?* It's a good question.

I have always loved dragonflies. I love the way they look—the way they glide and hover over water like helicopters. I also love the fact that they don't bite, because overall, I don't really like wasps and other insects that sting.

As I pondered an image to place on the cover, I wanted to use the dragonfly. You see, dragonflies are not only fascinating and gentle, but also they are symbols of change. Dr. Don Eisenhauer explains the dragonfly's process of change like this:

The word *metamorphosis* literally means change. Examples of metamorphosis include a tadpole changing into a bullfrog, or a caterpillar changing into a butterfly. Did you know that a dragonfly experiences the same kind of metamorphosis? Before it is changed into a dragonfly, it exists as a nymph (or water bug).

The nymph lives for one to three years under water. It is an ugly insect who bites and stings its prey. It is both mean and ugly! Eventually, after a few years in this condition, the nymph finds itself climbing up the stalk of a lily pad. Before long it experiences a change. The ugly, mean, underwater nymph is transformed into a beautiful, free, flying dragonfly.

In every way imaginable, what takes place is a change for the better. There are no comparisons between what the nymph was and what the dragonfly becomes. But just imagine what that change must be like for the nymph. The nymph knows nothing else besides his underwater home and his ugly body. To suddenly find himself changing, and moving from an existence in the water to a new existence in the air, must be terrifying. . . .

The symbolism of the dragonfly's story gives us hope in the midst of . . . change. It gives us hope that in spite of our fears; in spite of our lack of understanding; there is something far better to come.[1]

Like the dragonfly, God will bring you through seasons of change for your benefit and for your freedom. Don't resist it, and don't despise it. Change can be a blessing in disguise. God will use these seasons to refine us. As I often say: the call is free, the process is costly, but the rewards are priceless.

When He asks you to let go of an offense and release hurts

from the past, then obey His voice. The rewards will be internal peace and freedom, which are better than anything the world has to offer.

As for me, I was about to experience healing and find my true identity.

FINDING MY PURPOSE

Before I found freedom through forgiveness, I was often consumed with the heartache of what was happening at home. Our family issues seemed to get worse every year instead of better. We lived from one crisis to another. One night, while I was at home writing a paper and trying to study, I was overwhelmed with sadness from all the issues that kept piling up. I fell on my knees and pleaded with the Lord to fix my family and to make everything normal in my home. I was so sick of the fighting and the turbulence.

I was tired of the family dinner nights that turned into verbal boxing matches. I hated how sad my parents were all the time, which affected the atmosphere of our house. I was the only child still living at home at this time, yet it felt as if everyone's problems still lived with us. My parents were so preoccupied with my brothers that I didn't want to upset them or bother them with anything else, because it wouldn't have ended well for me. I had no one to talk to and felt very alone in my house.

I mentioned in the first chapter that the word *special* was spoken over my life as a newborn, but that word felt like a mockery to me. It seemed that this word would follow me all the days of my life repeating itself over and over, yet I could not accept the word as applicable to me. I was not special. I was unplanned. My family was far from special, so why on earth would people say that I was special? It was as if I had some sort of muffler on my ears that blocked me from receiving the word. The Enemy had distorted my understanding of who I was. The Lord was trying to tell me something, but I wasn't listening—until the night I cried out to God and asked Him: "Why was I born? Why put me in this situation when I wasn't even wanted?"

I blamed God for everything I was going through. Even though I was a Christian—and studying to be a minister—deep down, I felt hopeless and did not want to live anymore. I lay on the floor and wept bitterly, wondering if I would ever amount to anything in my life. I had made so many mistakes, I had no idea who I was and why I was here; I felt aimless. I was studying to become a minister, but I felt like a fraud. I was trying to do all the right things because I thought maybe if I earned the title of pastor and had a title on my door, then I would finally feel as though I had a purpose and people would affirm and respect me. Maybe if I could help someone else's problems, then doing so would diminish my own.

At that moment of desperation, I knew I needed an answer from God. The Bible says, "You will seek me and find me when you seek me with all your heart" (Jeremiah 29:13). I began seeking God because He was my only option. I opened the Bible and read this passage of Scripture as tears rolled down my cheeks.

> For you created my inmost being;
> you knit me together in my mother's womb.
> I praise you because I am fearfully and wonderfully made;

your works are wonderful,

I know that full well.

My frame was not hidden from you

when I was made in the secret place,

when I was woven together in the depths of the earth.

Your eyes saw my unformed body;

all the days ordained for me were written in your book

before one of them came to be. (Psalm 139:13–16)

The Enemy had pierced my heart every time he repeated the lie that I was not wanted: *Why are you here? You are just a nuisance. You're stupid.* These words shaped how I viewed myself for the next two decades. Yet while reading Psalm 139, a warmth that felt like healing oil moved through my body. I felt as if I was being held in the arms of my Creator, who was whispering the truth into my ear. Every word of Scripture was destroying every lie that was ever spoken over my heart and mind. I was being set free by God's Word.

In that moment, I realized that God used my parents to get me here, but God my Father had always planned for me to be here. He knew me. He saw me. He knit every fiber of who I am in the secret place where no one else could see. He was writing my future in His book before I took my first breath. He chose me to be His and to leave a mark on this earth—the kind of mark that no one can make but me. It was as if the scales had fallen from my eyes, and I could see clearly for the first time.

I wept for hours that night, leaving behind every evil word that was meant to poison me. The Enemy had a plan to kill, steal, and destroy me (John 10:10)—but I discovered the secret to who I truly was. I was a daughter who belonged to my Father God. It was time to allow Him to go to the deepest recesses of my heart and heal every wound and every word. He needed to replace Satan's lies with His truth. I read Psalm 139 over and over again until it became my truth. These living words were sharper and more effective than any surgery (Hebrews 4:12), and they cut out the cancer of self-hate.

I felt different. I felt clean, and for the first time I felt special. I felt special because even though I was a surprise to my parents, God had me in mind before the foundations of the earth. So now I had a reason to live: to discover my purpose according to Psalm 139:16, which says God had all of my days ordained to mean something. Specifically, it says, "all the days ordained for me were written in your book"—so I had to study the book He gave me, which is His Word. To walk in true freedom, I had to renew my mind. I had to transform the old patterns of thinking with new patterns of thinking, and the only way I could do that was by meditating on scriptures that declared the opposite of what had been spoken over my life for years. I had to replace every lie with God's truth until it became my normal pattern of thinking.

The Bible is clear when it says: "Do not conform to the pattern of this world, but be transformed by the renewing of your mind. Then you will be able to test and approve what God's will is—his good, pleasing and perfect will" (Romans 12:2). Instead of conforming to what feels most natural or familiar according to our feeling and emotions, we need to renew our minds daily in the Word of God and God's way of thinking. This can only happen as we spend time reading and meditating on His Word, pondering over and over what it means and how it applies to our lives. This will change the way we view ourselves and others, and it will also change how we behave.

There is a reason why people hurt others. It is because they are hurt and broken on the inside. Once I received healing by forgiving my mother, I could see her through a different lens. The lens I now looked through was one of love and forgiveness, which helped me comprehend how my mother had been a victim of abuse and negativity from her own mother. I understood that her actions toward me were not against me personally. It was a generational pattern that had not been broken, and I had to decide to put a stop to the cycle of control, manipulation, anger, fear, emotional breakdown, and gossip.

I am weary of seeing men and women who are bound up by their circumstances, refusing to let go of their pride and hurt in order to find freedom. You can do all things through Christ, who gives you strength (Philippians 4:13). The Holy Spirit is at work in your life. You just have to choose whether to obey His will or yours. It's that simple.

THE PROCESS TAKES TIME

I used to think that arriving at my dream destination would solve all my problems. When I go on that vacation, I will finally feel rested. When I leave home, I will be free of issues. When I get the dream job, then I will feel secure. When I get married, I will feel complete. When I have a family, I will feel whole.

I have now come to realize that the destination never delivers what we think it will deliver. We find ourselves arriving at the so-called destination only to discover that the ache and longings in our hearts are still there. Frustrated and perplexed, we continue on this rabbit trail of trying to find true happiness. We continue to do the same things over and over, and we find ourselves exhausted and disappointed with the One who has all the answers for our quest to discover who we are and why we are here.

God is much more interested in who we are becoming than in what we are achieving. We need to remember that it takes time to develop and create something valuable. We must become content in whatever stage we find ourselves in. We need to trust that the journey helps shape and mold us into who we are becoming. The journey needs to become the destination, because God's timing to bring about our dreams and desires is always perfect.

The process of discovering your true identity includes many stages. Many moments of transition and many experiences of growth and change will take place during your faith journey. Our walk with God is a marathon, not a sprint. Therefore, we must remind ourselves that each lap takes time, but we are being changed from the inside out.

If we focus on the negative, then our outcome will be negative too. But if we focus on the positive, our perspective changes and hope fills our hearts, even when circumstances look bad. This is why the Bible urges us to, "[Fix] our eyes on Jesus, the pioneer and perfecter of faith" (Hebrews 12:2). When we choose to look through the lens of Jesus, we see through eyes of hope. That was what took place in me. Every day was a directed step forward in my transformation from hurt to healed.

The apostle Paul understood this all too well. He knew he was being changed from glory to ever-increasing glory (2 Corinthians 3:18), and the work that Christ had begun in him was going to be brought to completion through Christ, who first promised it (Philippians 1:6). Paul would not have been able to accomplish what he did without the adversity and challenges that came his way. Amid those challenges, he learned how to exercise the faith, perseverance, love, and humility that come from knowing Jesus intimately.

I do not enjoy the process, and I have often looked at the process as a painful waste of time. We all just want to get to the finish line—to the fulfillment of our dreams and to the end of our stories. But it's through the process that we discover who we truly are. For example, the apostle Paul knew exactly who he was. He was an apostle, a teacher, and a servant of Christ. But before he had an encounter with Jesus, he was a murderer who believed in the cause of preserving the Old Testament truths. He was an expert who knew the Jewish law like the back of his hand, yet God called him to be an apostle to the Gentiles, who had no idea of Jewish traditions. Paul had to overcome certain labels that were given to him; he also had to shake off the guilt of the crimes he had committed. God had to take Paul through the process to discovering who he truly was. We have each been given a measure of grace (Ephesians 4:7), and we need to operate within that measure. You may not be able to do everything someone else can, but you have a unique gifting that no one else does.

Knowing who we are *not* parallels the alteration process

too. God removes the extra fabric that does not fit the measurements of your destiny in Him. Sometimes the alteration process looks like snipping fabric away. For me, the alteration process has been about removing the heavy drapes of unforgiveness and the lies by which I was living. Ejecting these from my life's fabric has facilitated further beauty and opened the door to finding out who I truly am.

Our Master Tailor cuts away the excess cloth because He envisions His completed design. He must cut away the unnecessary things that we have accumulated along the way so that we become what He has planned for us to be.

Dear Lord,

Thank You for being involved in every part of my life, despite how much I might feel You have abandoned me during those seasons when I was being molded and reshaped. I know Your timing is perfect, and You are the only One who knows when it is the right time to cut away the extra fabric. Forgive me for the times I misunderstand Your tailoring process. Help me remember that You are good and that You discipline those You love. I praise You because I know Your intent is to draw the best out of me when it will have the most impact in my life.

In Your name, amen.

CHAPTER TEN

HISTORY REPEATS ITSELF

The definition of insanity is doing the same thing
over and over again, but expecting different results.
—Source unknown

It wasn't until I became an adult that I realized I had taken
on many of my family's generational patterns. For so many
years, I had vowed that I would never be like my mother or
father in certain areas of my life—yet as an adult, I found myself
doing the exact things I loathed. As I continued to grow in my
faith and to seek healing in these areas, I understood that my
personal issues went deeper than I had known. I was continually
coming back to the same problem. It caused me to ask, *Why
does this always happen to me?* and *Why do I keep doing this?*

One pattern that was ingrained in me was sabotaging

relationships. I would end a friendship before the other person could hurt me, moving on due to my insecurities and fear of being rejected. Even though I wanted things to change, I had no clue where to begin. Also, I was irrationally angry all the time. I would feel a burning anger rising up in me. I wanted to hit things and scream at others when that trigger was hit.

I became an aunty at fourteen years of age. My older siblings had seven children between them during a ten-year period, so for all my teenage life, I was surrounded by their children. I remember getting so enraged with my nieces and nephews whenever they got out of hand that I would yell at them and want to spank them, and it scared me to death. My anger felt uncontrollable, and I didn't know what to do with it. I swore to myself that I wouldn't have kids of my own because I feared harming them. Little did I know at the time that this was a generational pattern throughout my mother's side of the family.

GOD'S PATTERN FOR US

Patterning is the most important step of designing a garment. If the pattern is incorrectly drawn, then the finished product will not function as it was designed to function. Therefore, the tailor must alter the pattern and create the garment according to the correct design.

In order for a designer to create a garment that fits and works perfectly, the pattern must be drawn according to exact specifications. Normally the designer dreams up an idea and then sketches it on paper. The pattern is then made, and the tailor follows the instructions and sews accordingly.

God is our Master Tailor. He has given us a perfect pattern for our lives, and we should follow His instructions accordingly. These instructions can be found in the Bible. Worldly patterns produce damage and destruction to the garment, but godly patterns produce life and strength.

Reading the Word and allowing it to renew our minds will bring light to our negative patterns and show us how to create new and healthy ones. But first, let's spend some time looking at generational patterns and how we tend to repeat them.

GENERATIONAL PATTERNS

Did you grow up in a home in which your mother would yell and scream? Or with a father who had a problem with anger? If so, you may have vowed "I am never going to be like my mother" or "I will never act like my father"—but chances are good you grew up and did exactly what you did not want to do. Maybe you suffer from fear and anxiety, and you realize your parents and grandparents did as well.

Heredity influences how we look and how we behave. People say, "Like father, like son." History seems to repeat itself. Just as this is true in genetics, it is also true in the spiritual realm of our family line.

Some examples of generational curses can be family illnesses that are passed down from one person to the next: anxiety, alcoholism, eating disorders, sexual abuse, physical abuse, lust, anger, manipulation and control, constant financial difficulties, mental problems, addiction, adultery, and the list goes on. Anything that seems to be a persistent struggle or problem handed down from one generation to another may very well be a generational curse.

Just as we inherited the curse of sin from Adam and Eve through the generations, we also inherit the tendency to sin in the same way as our ancestors. We need to understand there is a cycle that needs to be broken, but until we are aware of generational patterns, the behavior will simply be accepted as family history or genetics. I don't believe we are supposed to settle for suffering through life with destructive behavior that continues for generations. There is always a root cause for these issues, and we have the power to break the cycle of negative patterns in our family line.

If we look closely, we will discover there are certain behavioral patterns that are ingrained us. We may not consider these patterns to be abnormal because we have never known any different, and we assume other families operate in the same way. Or maybe we recognize that this is a pattern over our lives, but we don't know how to break free from it.

Most of us will simply accept the cycle and assume things will always be this way. This faulty assumption sometimes gives us an excuse to lean into our bad patterns. However, we can break the cycle and change our behavior with God's help as He reveals what's truly at work in our lives.

MY FAMILY'S HISTORY REPEATING ITSELF

My parents were brought up in religious homes, restricted by the confines of tradition. Five years before I was born, they discovered Jesus in a whole new way. During those first few years of rediscovery, they were learning how to develop their personal relationships with God.

Although my parents had found Jesus Christ as their Savior, they still thought God was distant and would judge and condemn them if they ever messed up. When they did sin, they assumed they had to pay penance for their actions and make their way back into God's good graces. Even though they had received God's glorious free gift of salvation, they still had to learn how to walk out that freedom and the power that comes with it. There was so much from their past that had to be transformed.

As a child, I didn't understand that my parents had their own struggles, doubts, and insecurities. We often forget that our parents have their own issues to face. We think they should know everything because, let's face it, when we are children, we see them as superheroes! In reality, they were just navigating through life as we are now. My parents were simply replicating the patterns they had seen and experienced growing up.

My mum could be a kind and fun person who would laugh and dance and sing with us in the kitchen. We would waltz and sing opera at the top of our lungs until my father got annoyed and told us to stop. Yet other times, she could be cruel with her words. She would become irrational if we disobeyed her. I remember one time my brothers came home later than expected from riding their bikes in the neighborhood, and instead of reprimanding them in a normal way, my mum took an ax from the shed and began to chop at their bikes. We stood in fear, watching her take out her anger on these bikes and wondering what we were in for later. We never knew what mood she would be in at any given time. Because of that, we became increasingly insecure and afraid when our mum would lose her temper.

The pain of the generational anger that my mother carried went very deep. I thought it was my fault when my mother was upset. I thought if I just tried harder to be good or was quieter around the house, then maybe she wouldn't get frustrated with me. Maybe if I just let her control every situation, then she wouldn't think I was resisting.

At the time, I believed my mother's behavior was because of her frustration with us. I didn't realize there was a deeper issue that even she didn't know she had. In order to understand why my mum struggled with anger, we need to go back one more generation.

My grandmother experienced a loss that most people would find unable to bear. She watched her four-year-old son die in a tragic accident. If that wasn't devastating enough, she was not allowed to bury her son or give him a proper funeral, as the parish priest had deemed him "cursed" because he had died in an accident. A part of her was buried that day with him, and she was never the same again.

Bitterness and unforgiveness took root in her heart, which led to a pattern of anger. Her fury left lasting damage in its wake. For my mother, then, growing up was difficult. It was especially hard being a daughter to a mother who never healed from the death of her beloved son. Even though my mother was provided for, my grandmother used harsh words and a heavy hand to keep my mother under control. My grandmother repeatedly told her, "God took the good one and left me the child who is a constant thorn in my flesh." Those were the words spoken over my mother's life as a child, and she believed them. She then began to walk out those words.

Because she believed she was rebellious and wild, she *became* wild, outspoken, and deliberate in gaining attention. She would make her mother furious. She subconsciously tried to become the boy her mother had lost. My mum learned early on in life that men could do what they wanted whenever they wanted, whether it was good or bad. Men had all the freedom. Men were favored by their mothers and could do no wrong. So my mother learned to be the best farmhand and help to her father as if she was a son. She was rugged and quite the tomboy, but though there was a toughness about her, in her heart she longed to be loved and accepted.

Disappointments kept piling up in her life. My mother wasn't allowed to be educated beyond the fifth grade because, in the 1940s, women were conditioned to be house-wives. Education was seen as a waste of time for women. My mother was devastated because all she wanted to do was learn, and she dreamed about making a mark on her world. That opportunity was taken away from her, and she had to work on the farm. She had to live with the decision that was made for her.

Another disappointment that nearly broke my mother happened when she had to leave her country and venture to the other side of the world. The move from Italy to Australia heightened her feelings of inadequacy and rejection. She did not speak the native language and felt like a foreigner, isolated and unaccepted, which added to the rejection she already had experienced. At twenty-one, she married my father out of convenience, and the generational cycle and curse of disappointment, abuse, anger, and rejection continued through the years, becoming greater and more deeply ingrained.

All the skeletons of the past were locked up in the tight closet of her heart. She never spoke about her issues or pain, because in her day you never talked about your problems with anyone. Admitting you had a problem was shameful. Maybe she believed that everything would work out on its own. After two nervous breakdowns and a near divorce, my mom struggled for her freedom, and in the process, she made many mistakes in her parenting. She truly desired to be the best mother she could be, but she didn't know how to break the cycle. She was part of a community that kept up appearances, and no one dared talk about what was going on behind closed doors.

THE ONLY WAY TO FIND TRUE FREEDOM

It's important to know that things don't ever work themselves out on their own. The issues of the past need to be confronted head on and dealt with. We are all broken and fractured in some way, and the only way to find true freedom is to go directly to the One who made us and knows our past better than we do. He is the only One who has the power to work all things together "for the good of those who love him, who have been called according to his purpose" (Romans 8:28). The cycle of brokenness can stop if we allow God to heal our hurts and break the links in our generational chains.

The wounds from my childhood were the result of my parents' years of accumulated emotional baggage growing heavier and heavier, becoming worse over time because their issues were never spoken aloud—let alone dealt with. If people cannot even love themselves, then how on earth can they expect to love others? We try to draw from an account that is in deficit, and then we wonder why we get disappointed when we don't find anything there. Most broken people are bankrupt of emotion and empathy, which means they cannot possibly give out what they need themselves. The world is full of never-ending cycles of hurt people hurting people.

Thankfully, there is a way to break the cycle and forge a new path for future generations!

Jesus came "to bind up the brokenhearted, to proclaim freedom for the captives and release from darkness for the prisoners" (Isaiah 61:1). He came to bring freedom to the oppressed and healing to all who will receive it. He came to break every generational curse. The Enemy wants us to believe the lie that we can never be healed from the pain and damage that was done to us. But God's true Word says we can. There is no pain, no sin, no damage that God cannot heal. Psalm 147:3 says, "He heals the brokenhearted and binds up their wounds." We don't have to be slaves to the prison of pain, because God can give us "a crown of beauty instead of ashes" (Isaiah 61:3).

To fully change the faulty patterns that we have allowed in our lives, we must renew our minds with God's Word and allow His pattern to redeem our thoughts, which ultimately will change our behavior. He has given us an instruction manual—the Bible—to help rewrite our story. With God's help, we can live a purposeful life that will positively influence future generations.

CONFRONTING THE GENERATIONAL CURSES

During our first year of marriage, I had a disagreement with my husband, Henry, about how much money we should give one of his friends who was getting married. The groom-to-be was close to Henry but not so much to me, and I hadn't met his future wife. So when it came to deciding how much to put in the card, Henry wanted to put in more than I thought we should. He was being generous, and I was being stingy. Looking back now, it was the difference of about fifty dollars, but at the time it was a big deal because we were struggling financially.

We debated all the reasons for and against, and I kept raising my voice and becoming more and more irrational. At one point, while I was screaming at the top of my lungs, Henry said: "Stop this. This is stupid!" When I heard the word *stupid*, it was as if Henry had just pressed the red nuclear bomb release button—and I exploded. I was furious that Henry had just called me stupid (or so I thought). I hated being called *stupid* because that was the painful label that had been spoken over me—the word I had chosen to wear over my life for so many years.

When Henry pressed that button, all hell broke loose in our home. I screamed even louder and grabbed my keys and stormed out, slamming the door behind me and getting in my car to drive off as I had seen my mother do over the course of my childhood. I was so hurt and so angry with him that I needed to gather my thoughts and grab some ammunition to come back with. I couldn't control the irrational anger that came over me, and I wanted to lash out and hurt him as much as he had just hurt me. I said to myself: *See? It was always too good to be true. I knew he would hurt me one day, and here we are repeating history. Now my own husband is calling me stupid.* Henry tried calling my cell, but I stubbornly refused to answer. I wanted to punish him and ignore him for as long as I saw fit.

Well, I had nowhere to go but home after a while. So I made my way home. I planned to pick up from where we left off, and I would make Henry pay for what he had said. As I arrived home, I was ready for a fight—but something happened that changed my life forever. When I arrived at the door, there was a poster stuck on the glass. In bold pink writing it said:

Ten things I love about Alex:

1. I love how beautiful she is.
2. I love that she cooks crumbed chicken for me.
3. I love how she laughs.
4. I love how her hair falls around her face.
5. I love that she keeps the house so clean.
6. I love how she always puts others first.
7. I love how she worships God.
8. I love that she's smart and talented.
9. I love how creative she is.
10. I love that she is kind and funny.

Those words arrested me and brought me to my knees in tears. I had never been confronted with kindness after

I had said such awful things. All I had known was yelling, screaming, and fighting. Henry's poster and his kind words disarmed the bomb that was waiting to be detonated in front of him. I did not know how to respond. I was speechless. I walked in the door with the poster in hand and tears running down my face, and I was received with open arms. In a loving tone, Henry said: "I love you, Alex, and we are on the same team. We need to work things out as a couple, not as opponents. I don't know what triggered that behavior, but I am so sorry if I hurt you in any way. Are you able to tell me what I did or said that upset you so much?"

I burst into another wave of tears and said, "You called me stupid, and that hurt my heart." Henry replied: "Sweetheart, I did not call you stupid. I said this argument is stupid, and the way we were fighting about fifty dollars was so unnecessary. The fight had gotten way out of hand." We embraced.

After I sat down, I began to unpack what had happened in my heart. My irrational outburst of anger was a pattern of behavior that had been ingrained in me because it was what I had witnessed in my family growing up. Yelling and screaming was the language in our household. To be heard, we had to fight. Therefore, this situation—which looked all too familiar to me—triggered the unresolved issue in my heart of being called stupid. That word had dictated my life long enough, so when I heard it coming from my husband's mouth, I went into my default mode.

Now I realized this was a deeper issue. It was a generational pattern of irrational anger I had inherited from my mum. Henry and I navigated a few more of those outbursts until I finally received healing in my heart. I can honestly say that the unconditional love and kindness from my husband, who then journeyed alongside me as Jesus undertook my inner healing, finally erased those patterns in my life. I allowed the healing touch of Jesus to take away the sting of those words, and He replaced them with the truth that I was not stupid, but in fact smart and loved.

In my past, I had witnessed this behavior time and time again with my siblings. I saw the collateral damage done to my extended family members due to the verbal abuse and anger. This reinforced how broken our family was and how much it revealed that these behaviors were so ingrained in our thinking and pattern of living—I had believed there was no way out. I had felt I did not have the power to change at all. I had believed that these patterns were out of my control and because of what was done to me and said over me that it stained my heart forever.

I think sometimes we presume that transformation is impossible, that there is no hope for things to be different because the cycles of the past dictate our future. We move forward, saying, "If you can't beat them, join them." I believed Satan's lies inside my head were true; therefore, I just learned to cope with them and hope for the best. I have come to realize through much teaching and encountering God's presence that when Jesus died on the cross, He took every curse and all iniquity upon His shoulders and declared, "It is finished" (John 19:30). But we must come face-to-face with our issues and admit these strongholds will not go away by themselves. Only when we receive the tools to release them from our lives will we find the freedom on the other side of our breakthrough.

HOW TO FIND FREEDOM FROM GENERATIONAL PATTERNS

The good news is that freedom is possible! We can be released from these patterns and break the cycle of dysfunction and sin in our lives. The power of the blood of Jesus allows us to be free from every sin and iniquity that has been passed down from generation to generation. We need to acknowledge the problem and then bring it to Jesus—confessing, repenting, and receiving His love and forgiveness. These patterns in our lives can be broken through faith that the power of His blood is strong enough to remove all remnants of sin. His blood has the power to cancel any curse and to release His blessing.

A generational pattern comes through the bloodline of our earthly family, and the only way this generational pattern can be cancelled is through the blood of Jesus. We have been saved and set free by His blood, and we are now part of His bloodline. It's as simple as recognizing our out-of-control patterns and behaviors, bringing them before Jesus, and renouncing their power over our lives.

To *renounce* means to "formally declare one's abandonment of (a claim, right, or possession)."[1] The Bible says in James 5:16: "Confess your sins to each other and pray for each other so that you may be healed. The prayer of a righteous person is powerful and effective." Ask Jesus to reveal to you right now the patterns that are stopping you from living in the fullness of freedom, and then pray this prayer:

Dear Lord,
   I come before You in Jesus' name. I recognize the

power You have given me by Jesus' blood to demolish spiritual strongholds and generational patterns. I confess that I have given a foothold to the sins and iniquities of my family; therefore, I renounce and denounce every stronghold You have revealed to me by the authority and name of Jesus, according to Your Word.

I take back through the power of Jesus' blood the ground that I surrendered to the Enemy. I pray that You will remove every sin, fill me with the Holy Spirit, and help me conform to the image of Christ in every area of my life.

In Your name, amen.

CHAPTER ELEVEN

THE MAKE OR BREAK
OF CIRCUMSTANCES

Give thanks in all circumstances; for this
is God's will for you in Christ Jesus.
—1 Thessalonians 5:18

Three years into my marriage, I went to the doctor because I had not had a menstrual cycle for eleven months. It took me so long to make an appointment because I feared that I had damaged my body from starving it for so many years. I was frightened to face the possibility that because of neglecting my own body, I might be barren. After a series of tests, the results came back, and I was diagnosed with hyperprolactinemia. This condition is caused by a tumor on the pituitary gland at the base of the brain, which sends incorrect messages to the body's hormones and tricks the body into thinking it is pregnant when it isn't. The doctors told me it would be difficult to get pregnant because this is a form of infertility. They also told me that I would need to be on medication for the rest of my life to regulate my hormonal imbalance.

I was floored by the news. All I heard was: "You are *infertile*"—yet another label to add to the list. I could hardly believe it. I was angry that this was happening to me—after all, I had been a faithful servant of the Lord. I had kept myself pure; therefore, I deserved to be rewarded with children, right? Talk about being a self-righteous person! I viewed God as a taskmaster who rewarded "good Christian behavior."

My perception of how God treats us was completely incorrect; He doesn't reward our good Christian behavior with children. I was mad at God and wondered why I had this ridiculous condition that was so embarrassing to talk about, and I was angry that I had to endure the side effects that came with the medication. Why me? I began to feel sorry for myself. *Of course this would happen to me,* I'd think. It was another reminder of what a disappointment I was.

When I came home and told my husband about my condition, he stood firm in what he believed. He said we had no other option but to stand in faith, choosing not to accept my diagnosis as truth. As soon as we did that, we began the journey of faith toward seeing a miracle take place. Scientifically, it may have been a fact that I had this condition, but my Bible says that Jesus has "the name that is above every name" (Philippians 2:9). The name of *hyperprolactinemia* was under the name of Jesus because of what He did on the cross. The fact is, "by his wounds we are healed" (Isaiah 53:5). I stood on those words and stood in faith for my healing.

About a year later, I still had no healing and no baby. I was performing in an Easter production at my church, and one of the prayer team members asked if we could get together and pray. As we were praying about my infertility, she sensed that the Lord was giving her a word for me. The words were *inner vow*. She asked if I had ever made a vow about not having children. I asked the Holy Spirit to reveal if there were any vows I had made in the past.

As I sat there waiting for the Lord to speak, suddenly I had a flashback. I was sixteen years old, and my brothers both had children out of wedlock at a young age. Our family took them in, and some days it was chaotic in our household with so many babies crying and needing attention. The atmosphere made it difficult for me to concentrate and study, and I felt as though my teenage life was being robbed from me. I remembered feeling a false sense of responsibility to care for the children, and I was not happy about it at all.

I also remembered sitting at the dining room table trying to finish an assignment for school, but I couldn't concentrate due to the noise and commotion. I had just about had enough! I remember saying with such conviction in my heart: "I will never have children. They ruin your life, and I never want them!" I was mad and so resentful that I was having to deal with the poor choices that some of my family had made.

As soon as I remembered that vow, I repented and renounced the statement. I began to understand the power of our spoken words. I began to change my speech.

My husband and I practiced speaking out what we

imagined having in our lives. We began talking about what our children would look like and what they would be like. When talking about our future children, we would say, "*When* we have kids," not "*If* we have kids." We would describe what we wanted them to look like and what they would be like. We began making declarations of faith. I started using words to bless my womb, instead of to curse it.

It was a two-year faith journey until we had our first child, but I firmly believe repenting of the childhood vow I had made was a significant turning point in my healing. Now we have our beautiful daughter, Holly, and our son, Taylor, who are exactly what we had imagined before they were even born. Henry and I even prayed that they would have magnetic blue eyes and golden curly hair, and they do—even though neither of us has blue eyes. Every time people comment on my children's blue eyes, I tell them the story of God's miraculous power and His faithfulness to His promise. He receives all the glory for not only healing my womb, but also for going above and beyond to answer the desires of my heart.

Are you in a situation that looks impossible at the moment? Maybe you are single and longing to meet your spouse. Maybe you have a diagnosis that has interrupted your life. Or perhaps you have been carrying a dream in your heart for so long that it doesn't look as though it will ever come to pass. You might be walking through something you never thought you would, such as the death of a loved one. We may think that God is holding out on us, but God wants to remind us of His nature: He is a good Father who loves us, and He wants us to know the truth. Because when we know the truth, it will set us free (John 8:32).

WORSHIP THROUGH THE PAIN

How do we reconcile that God is good when situations in our lives are going bad? How do we not believe God has let us down when He doesn't answer our prayers when we cry out to Him? How do we trust a God who says He will answer us when it feels as though He hasn't yet?

Some of the most stressful times in life are when you go through a major change, such as moving houses, moving cities, experiencing death in your family, or having a child. These events can be overwhelming and require major adjustments, both emotionally and physically. In 2002, the bottom of my world fell out from under me. Not only did I go through some of the greatest losses I have ever experienced, but also every single one of those items listed above took place in my life during a two-year period.

I was serving God faithfully and navigating through this season of belief for a miracle in my womb. If that wasn't stressful enough, I learned from a phone call that the closest person to my heart died unexpectedly. My beautiful cousin, who was more like a sister to me, died suddenly at the age of twenty-nine with no warning! She was gone, just like that. This was the first time I had ever tasted the death of a loved one, and I was devastated. *How could this happen to her? Why did this happen to her? Why didn't God save her life?*

Sometimes as Christians, we presume we are exempt from bad things happening to us or our loved ones when we are following the rules and walking in faith. I have counseled many people who love God with all their hearts, and the question they repeat over and over is, "Why did God let this happen?" There I was, asking the same question: *Is God still good even when things go bad?* Yes, He is! Bad things happen to good people because we live in a fallen and broken world. It is the very reason that God had to send Jesus—to save us from ourselves. We follow our own will and our own choices, which have obviously not been great choices. Then we blame God when things go bad, and we thank Him when things are great.

The day I found out that my cousin had died, I was on tour with our worship team in another state. We were scheduled to worship at a church in a small country region of Victoria. We were driving along having a good time when I received the devastating phone call. I was overcome with grief. Thank God my husband was with me in the car. I fell into his arms and wept bitterly. We arrived at the church, but I wanted to be home with my family. I couldn't even stand up due to the shock of this heartbreaking news. My pastor said I could sit out this worship service and just take it easy, as she understood this was too much for me to handle. I agreed that I would be a blubbering mess if I got up on that stage, but then I sensed God's voice saying, *Sing your way through your pain.*

Sing? I thought. *I can't even get two words out right now without bawling my eyes out.*

I sensed it again: *Sing, Alex. Worship your way through the pain.*

I told the team I wanted to sing because I felt I had to. And I discovered that night that, though there is power when we worship when all is well in our world, there is another level of breakthrough when we choose to declare that God is good even when our circumstances are not. I chose to worship in my darkest moment and give God glory regardless of my circumstances.

As I got onstage that night, the worship that poured out of

my heart was pure incense to God. The sacrifice of my praise unlocked my heart (Hebrews 13:15), and I worshiped God in Spirit and truth (John 4:24). I was hurting and distraught, but I chose to come to God with that pain instead of running away from Him and isolating myself. I wasn't pretending to have it all together when I came to Him; I came broken because I knew God could handle my questions and my pain. He knew exactly how I was feeling and was the only One who could heal my heart. I stood there defenseless and vulnerable, and as I worshiped, the presence of God fell over the entire congregation. Many years later I revisited that church, and the people who were there that night still remember how profound the presence of God was that evening. My worship was raw and authentic—just the way God likes it.

I learned during that season that God is good all the time, despite the outcome. He taught me how to break through the feeling of being overcome with sadness and how to replace those feelings with worship and the Word. I found God in the secret place of my prayer closet, which helped me in every area of my life. I had struggled with depression, hopelessness, and shame, but when I learned how to pursue God, I discovered what freedom truly looks like.

CAST YOUR CARES ON GOD

First Peter 5:7–9 says: "Cast all your anxiety [cares] on him because he cares for you. Be alert and of sober mind. Your enemy the devil prowls around like a roaring lion looking for someone to devour. Resist him, standing firm in the faith."

I have learned that the way to resist the Enemy—who wants to take your life into a downward spiral—is by casting your cares on the One who truly cares for you. I developed an acronym for the word *CARES* that gave me the keys for breakthrough when my life was at its darkest points. What the enemy means to break you with, God will use to help you break through.

C: Cry Out

Someone very special to me experienced a tragedy years ago when her son was rushed to the ER. He was misdiagnosed, which resulted in him dying on arrival at the hospital. He was resuscitated back to life, but during that process he lost oxygen to his brain, which caused serious damage. Afterward, she said these words I will never forget: "Alex, when adversity comes to us, the first thing we need to do is cry a river." I had been taught to scrape together more faith, but she spoke words of wisdom when she said it is okay to cry.

I began to think about people in the Bible who cried: David in the Psalms cried; Hannah, who desperately wanted a child, cried; Job cried out because he had lost everything. Then I came across this scripture that made it real for me. Psalm 56:8 says: "You keep track of all my sorrows. You have collected all my tears in your bottle. You have recorded each one in your book" (NLT). Wow! What a beautiful picture of how good our God is. It's okay to cry, but we are not called to live there. We must get up after our mourning, and if we haven't seen a breakthrough yet, we take the next step in faith.

A: Appeal to God's Nature

To appeal means to make an application to a higher court for a decision to be reversed. When someone has been given a sentence in a court of law that is unjust, they can make an appeal to the judge, who has the power to overrule the verdict. When the evidence of truth is brought forth, the judge can bring freedom to the innocent. God the Father is our Judge, and He has the power to overrule a diagnosis and a negative situation. Therefore, when you pray, tell yourself and the Enemy that all God's promises are yes and amen (2 Corinthians 1:20). Declare Scripture over your life. The truth of God's Word will overrule the lies of the Enemy. Appeal to God, who is our just Judge and has the power to overrule what the Enemy has done. We can appeal to Him and ask Him to reverse the Enemy's verdict over our lives.

R: Remember Past Miracles

Pastor and author Charles Swindoll once said, "So often, when facing our own giants, we forget what we ought to remember and we remember what we ought to forget."[1] How true is that? We focus on all the things God hasn't done for us yet, and we forget to record all the wonderful miracles He has done. Psalm 103:2–6 says: "Praise the LORD, my soul, and forget not all his benefits—who forgives all your sins and heals all your diseases, who redeems your life from the pit and crowns you with love and compassion, who satisfies your desires with good things so that your youth is renewed like the eagle's. The LORD works righteousness and justice for all the oppressed." Don't forget what God has done. Remember that if He did it then, He will do it again. Keep a list of all the miracles He has given you. My husband once said to me, "If God never gave us another thing after our salvation, it would still be more than we ever deserved." Give thanks, because a grateful heart precedes miracles.

E: Enlarge God Over Your Circumstances

When we stop staring at our situations and choose instead to look up to the heavens into the face of Jesus, we realize that He is a big God; what looks like a mountain to us is merely a speck to Him. When we enlarge God over our circumstances, we are saying; "You are the God of the impossible, so I choose to let go of my worry and fear. I place it in Your hands because with You all things are possible."

S: Sing Through Your Pain

Isaiah 54:1 says, "'Sing, barren woman, you who never bore a child; burst into song, shout for joy, you who were never in labor; because more are the children of the desolate woman than of her who has a husband,' says the LORD." Singing through the pain will change the atmosphere of your life and cause breakthrough. Praise to God is incense to Him, but when we whine and complain instead of singing and praising, it is incense to the Enemy. The Enemy's kryptonite is when we worship God through adversity. Satan can't stand our praise because we are saying that God is good all the time regardless of our circumstances. When we choose to praise instead of complain, God releases His angel army to fight on our behalf and bring the breakthrough. Your circumstances may not change immediately, but *you* will change in that moment as you choose to sing over your pain.

146

When we decide not to lower God to our experiences on earth, we acknowledge His rightful place as God. It's only then that we discover His true nature, which enables us not to waver in unbelief, but to stand firm in the knowledge that God is good and that our stories are not finished yet. What the Enemy means for evil, God will turn around and use for good.

Why don't you take a moment right now and cast your cares on God by using the acronym *CARES*? Cry out, appeal to God's nature, remember the past miracles, enlarge God over your circumstances, and sing until you feel a shift in your heart. Before long, hope will overwhelm your soul.

Dear Lord,

I cast all my cares on You, knowing that You care for me. No matter what circumstances I am going through, I will cry out to You, appeal to Your nature, remember the miracles You have done for me in the past, enlarge You over my circumstances, and then sing my praises to You. You are good all the time, regardless of my circumstances. Thank You for loving me and leading me into Your truth.

In Your name, amen.

CHAPTER TWELVE

OUR PERSPECTIVE
MAKES THE DIFFERENCE

As the heavens are higher than the earth,
so are my ways higher than your ways
and my thoughts than your thoughts.
—Isaiah 55:9

When Henry and I were going through a difficult season in our ministry, we received some wise advice
that helped us understand the process a little better. A pastor
said to us: "A teacher never speaks to you while you're taking
a test, because they need you to apply what they have been
teaching you in theory. Now it needs to become practical."

Adversity can be a test of how well we know the character

and nature of God. He will use what the Enemy meant for evil and turn it around into something good. In that season, our adversity can either make us better or bitter—and it's our perspective that makes all the difference. Our understanding of the nature of our heavenly Father helps us navigate life's difficult situations. When the Enemy attacks your belief in God's character, he hopes you will lose faith in God and fail. Pressure will always reveal what is inside of you.

We are called to persevere during our tests of faith. As a result of these tests, we learn how to endure whatever trials we may face without losing our faith in God. This endurance comes from a faith that triumphs to the end, even during suffering. James 1:2–4 tells us: "Consider it pure joy, my brothers and sisters, whenever you face trials of many kinds, because you know that the testing of your faith produces perseverance. Let perseverance finish its work so that you may be mature and complete, not lacking anything."

The Bible includes a promise for those who stand in the middle of chaos, pain, and adversity—those who choose not to run away or wallow in self-pity, but instead to hold on and believe God. God promises to renew your strength, and when you think you cannot take one more breath, He will give you enough to keep going. He will hold tight to you even when you let go of Him. Isaiah 40:30–31 says: "Even youths grow tired and weary, and young men stumble and fall; but those who hope in the LORD will renew their strength. They will soar on wings like eagles; they will run and not grow weary, they will walk and not be faint."

You may be in a situation in which your faith is being tested in various ways. Maybe you are a mother who has been praying for an unsaved child for many years, or a wife whose husband has left you. Perhaps you are going through a financial struggle or a sickness that has been labeled terminal. Whatever your situation may be, God is more than able to reach down in the midst of your mess and rescue you from the pit.

THE IN-BETWEEN SEASON

Several years ago, the Lord reminded my heart about a dream He had placed in my spirit through one of my friends. She said she felt God say that I was about to birth something that had been in my heart for a long time, and that when it came to life, it would be more beautiful than I could have imagined. I remember thinking: *Thank You, Jesus. I am now going to do all those things You promised I would do—everything you spoke to me about all those years ago.* You see, I had always had a dream to teach and preach the word of God and write books. This was something I held deep in my heart and only shared with my husband. I also had a dream to serve God alongside my husband, because up until then we served in different areas of ministry and hardly got to minister as a couple. I couldn't work out in my mind how these dreams would come to pass.

As soon as I received this confirming whisper from God, I started planning—because surely God had spoken and we had to act NOW! How could I get the ball rolling? And so I began talking to my husband about it. I began to think through the logistics of it all, including how I could finish my current position at work and begin living out my dreams. I became convinced that God would work everything out within the next few weeks.

Well, nothing happened in the weeks following. Actually, nothing happened for the next two years. I was so frustrated because it seemed as if I was taking steps backward instead of moving forward. The dream in my heart seemed so far removed from me and completely out of grasp. I began to panic and take my stress out on everyone around me. I began to blame those who were closest to me, as if it was their fault I wasn't fulfilling my God-given dream. I also resented those around me who were living out their destinies.

One day, I became so burdened with what was *not* happening in my life that I gave up. I had allowed disappointment to come in and was looking at the situation through a filter of defeat and rejection. I felt the Lord whisper to me to take a drive to pray and worship Him. After some procrastinating, I finally got into the car and went for a drive. I was extremely distracted, and my mind was full of clutter and noise.

At a certain point in the drive, I calmed down and began to really worship, giving my burdens over to the Lord. I then felt Him clearly saying to me, *Alex, do you remember when you were pregnant with Holly?* I replied, "How could I forget!?" My doctor had given me a due date of May 14, but I had decided that I was going to give birth earlier than my due date. At this stage in life I was still struggling with an eating disorder and had been for nineteen years. As a result, I missed out on the joy of my first pregnancy. I lived every day of that pregnancy hating my body because of how it was growing. In my distorted mind, I saw my body as fat instead of focusing on the miracle in my womb. All I saw was a big bottom, huge thighs, and a chubby face.

I really disliked my body looking so pregnant. I was in a hurry to get back into my skinny jeans. When my due date came and went and I still hadn't delivered my baby, I was furious. Every day I would cry and whine to my husband. When I made an appointment with my doctor, I distinctly remember turning on the tears more than usual, trying to manipulate him into inducing me right away. He conceded and allowed me to be induced. I was over the moon, of course. I could finally pick the date and prepare to bring this baby into the world. I was in control! (Or so I thought.)

When Friday morning came, I was at the hospital by seven a.m. What should have been the most joyous day was quite possibly the worst day of my life. I was in labor for twenty-three hours, and every single thing I did not want to happen, happened. I was in extreme pain because the epidural was not administered properly and did not work completely. If that wasn't bad enough, I couldn't push my baby out and had to have a forceps delivery, which included an episiotomy. I was so exhausted and frustrated with the process that I didn't have any energy to nurse the baby when she was born. I just wanted to sulk and sleep. I truly believe this all took place because it was *my* plan to get this baby out early.

God then asked me to remember my second birth with Taylor a few years later. This time the doctor was a lot wiser and didn't give in to my manipulation. I went past my due date again. Henry was on tour in the United States at that time, while we were still living in Australia. I begged for the baby to be delivered a week or two early so Henry could be home for the delivery, but the doctor said no! He would not budge. He said we would wait for the baby to come in his time and not ours.

As it turned out, Henry arrived home two days before I went into labor. I wasn't even aware that I was in labor on the day that Taylor was born until I went in for my scheduled checkup and the doctor said I was already dilated five centimeters. Four hours later, I delivered my son without any pain relievers. I pushed twice, and Taylor was born. No forceps and no episiotomy! Just pure enjoyment to nurse him when he was given to me. What a difference!

I learned my lesson about trying to force God's hand. I had tried to make my dreams come true because of my lack of trust that God would do what He said He would do in my life. To be honest, I was a control freak who wanted to direct my own destiny. I was impatient that God wasn't birthing my dream as quickly as I wanted Him to.

As I drove in the car that day, God spoke to me ever so gently in my heart: *Awakening something before its time can be disastrous. If I open the doors for these dreams prematurely when you have not developed on the inside, then the very dream that is meant to nourish you and those around you will actually crush you, because you will not be able to carry the weight of responsibility that comes with promotion. Allow Me to birth the dream that is inside you in My time.*

I understood that my ways are not God's ways. His ways are higher, His thoughts are so much better, and His timing is always perfect (Isaiah 55:9). I repented of my attitude and impatience and cried the whole way home. I chose to trust in God's timing, and I allowed Him to do what He needed to do inside of me before releasing me into the destiny He had predestined before I was born.

So once again God was perfecting the work He began in me so that He could refine my character and develop my skills through pruning. During that season He taught me how to worship in the waiting period. God knew the steps we needed to take in the future, yet we were still unaware that God was about to require us to take a huge leap of faith.

REPLACING LIES WITH TRUTH

The process of healing the wounds in my heart didn't happen overnight. I had to learn to wait on God and get to know Him personally. Over time, I allowed Him to speak into my heart and replace the lies with His truth.

Here are some of the keys I used to unlock these areas in my heart:

Read the Word of God

Instead of picking up the phone and telling a friend or getting in my car and crying my eyes out, I chose to read the Word every time something negative happened to me. I read the Bible until something resonated in my heart. At times reading the Word felt like chewing glass, but instead of giving up, I pushed through. I kept reading until a word or a sentence caught my attention and spoke life into my heart. God always came through with a scripture that touched me, encouraging my healing to take place. I discovered such revelation and truth that those scriptures still resonate with me when I read them.

Get to Know God

We may know about God, but getting to know Him is entirely different. During my struggles, I got on my face in my bedroom and listened to worship music until I felt a breakthrough. Worship enlarged God over my situation and fed my spirit, which in turn increased my faith. Little by little, I felt closer to God, and healing took root in my heart. As I grew in relationship with Him, I began to leave the hurt on the floor and not pick it up again. I learned how to remain vulnerable and how to apply the Word of God in my life.

Listen to and Obey the Holy Spirit

The Holy Spirit is described as the "Comforter, Advocate, Intercessor—Counselor, Strengthener, Standby" (John 14:26 AMP). Jesus said that the Holy Spirit will teach us all things. We need to learn how to hear His voice, because He will ask you to do things and challenge your thinking. We have a choice to obey the Holy Spirit or not, but I guarantee you that His advice will help bring the healing and freedom you need in your life.

When I was eleven years old, I learned to hear the Holy Spirit's still, small voice inside my heart. When I did something wrong, I felt a slight tug in my heart. Some people call it a conscience, but I learned to lean in and trust that inner voice as God's Holy Spirit. He would tell me things that were key to seeing situations in my life turn around. If we learn to listen to the Holy Spirit's voice and obey His instructions, doing so will have a huge impact in our lives.

Be Willing to Forgive

During Bible college, I had to face my fears and restore my relationship with my mum. During that first year, when I discovered the truth of who I was, I was still living at home. Even though I had changed, my mum hadn't in certain areas.

One day, I remember sensing that I needed to buy her a gift. She loved porcelain ornaments, and I found this beautiful porcelain dog that looked like the dog my mother had growing up. I was sure her heart would be moved as I gave her this gift that had cost me and caused me to be vulnerable. I remember walking up to her in the kitchen and handing her the little wrapped gift. Her response was, "What's this?" I said nervously, "It's a gift for you." She said: "Why did you buy me a gift? I don't want a gift. It's just an extra thing that I need to dust. Why didn't you save your money?"

I wanted to grab that gift and smash it on the ground in front of her and call her every explicit name I could muster in that moment. I couldn't believe it. *Are you kidding me?* I was furious. As I stood there feeling shame and anger, I felt the Holy Spirit say, *Forgive her again.* Oh, how hard that command was in that moment. *Forgive her? Did You just see what happened? She is cruel and mean! This is why I can't deal with her.* Then the Lord pressed on my heart again and said, *Forgive her.*

I took the gift back because she didn't want it, and I went to my room and cried a river. I handed over my hurt to God. He said: *Continue to forgive her, even if you need to do it seventy times seven times. Your mother is hurt, and she doesn't know how to receive. You have received healing, so you need to continue to love her even when she continues to say hurtful things and push your gifts aside.*

In that moment, something in me changed. Now when I give love to someone, I choose to love them expecting nothing in return, because sometimes people are so broken that they are unable to receive the love you are offering. I discovered what unconditional love was.

Pray

I had to learn how to apply what God was showing me to my everyday life. I had to learn how to go to God and present my requests to Him. The Bible says: "Do not be anxious about anything, but in every situation, by prayer and petition, with thanksgiving, present your requests to God. And the peace of God, which transcends all understanding, will guard your hearts and your minds in Christ Jesus" (Philippians 4:6–7). Prayer is powerful, and it shifts atmospheres and circumstances. So instead of complaining and criticizing, pray to the One who can change you as well as the situation around you. Praying to God is talking to Him and sharing your heart. He doesn't need your eloquence; He just wants to be in a relationship with you. Begin talking to Him in your private time just as you would talk to a close friend, and then take a minute to listen and hear the thoughts that He places in your heart.

God carries us through times in which we simply cannot make it happen in our own strength. Learn to wait and be patient, for what God has begun He will bring to completion (Philippians 1:6). I had to surrender to the process. I had to repent for being angry about God's timing, and I had to release control over to Him to do what He needed to do in my life.

Why don't you take a moment and pray this prayer?

Dear Lord,

I repent for being frustrated with the process. Even though I can't see that anything is happening, I choose to believe that You are working behind the scenes on my behalf and that Your timing is perfect. I choose to surrender to Your process, and I give You permission to perfect what You have begun in me and bring it to completion. I choose to trust You. During this season, I ask You to draw me closer to Your heart, so that I may know You better. I love You.

In Your name, amen.

CHAPTER THIRTEEN

FROM DESERT TO DESTINY

It is in your moments of decision
that your destiny is shaped.
—Tony Robbins[1]

Have you ever had an off-season? Perhaps it came in the form of writer's block or a creative void, or a time when you were not creating something big. Sometimes off-seasons are necessary for God to draw out what He wants from us. Creative people work harder during the off-season than they do when the season is in full force. What you see in public is the result of what took place in private. The preparation phase—the time when mistakes are made and goals are set—matters most. What you do in private becomes a sight to behold in public. You are then free to reveal what has been created in confidence during the on-season, because you have prepared during the off-season. The Lord will open doors that no one else can, so it is important to be ready when God presents those opportunities to you.

A LONG JOURNEY TO THE PROMISED LAND

I did not see my personal off-season for what it was initially. God had called my husband and me to what I thought was going to be the promised land. He had been prompting our hearts to leave Australia and move to America for over a year. It was in a church service where I felt God whisper in my heart, "Are you prepared to go to *nothing* with *nothing* but My presence?" I remember feeling scared at the very thought of leaving behind everything I had ever known, including a church I had served in and helped build for decades—all to go far away with no job, no church, and no friends. Could that really have been the voice of God?

At that moment, the idea of stepping out in faith scared the life out of me, so I answered by saying, "Lord, I don't know if I have faith for that." Over the next little while, God continued to confirm this word of us moving our family to the other side of the world. We had no idea what He was calling us to do there, but we felt strongly that we needed to go. So we asked the Lord for one more sign.

Our pastors at the time suggested that if this was God, we should ask Him to confirm His direction by applying for the green card lottery that grants you free, permanent residency in the United States. If we won that lottery, we could take it as a sign that we were meant to go in faith and that the Lord would open the doors of our destiny when we arrived. That was in June of 2010, and the diversity Visa lottery did not open until October. Also, we applied to that lottery along with fourteen million other people, so the odds were not in our favor.

More waiting, I thought to myself. But what I didn't realize is that God was about to strengthen my faith muscle over this next season; He knew we were about to embark on the craziest faith journey we had ever been on, and we needed to be trained and ready. Fast-forward eleven months, and the day arrived to see if God had confirmed His word about us moving to the United States. I went to the computer, punched in my application code, and low and behold—we did not win the Visa lottery. "What?" I checked again because surely I had typed in the wrong details. Nope! The numbers were correct; we didn't get in.

My heart sank and I just wept. I said: "God, I thought you spoke to me. I am so confused right now." I called Henry, who was on tour in Germany at the time, and told him the news. Together we believed that God would make things clear. If His plan was for us to stay in Australia, we were okay with that. But a week later Henry returned home from Europe and told me about an email he had received from the US State Department explaining there had been a computer error while the lottery was being drawn. Because of that error, they had to redraw the lottery at a later date. I remember at that moment thinking: *God, You did this for us. We are going to America!*

Sure enough, on July 15, 2011, our family won the green card lottery. Wow! God made a way, and the whole thing was confirmation in the most miraculous way that we were called to GO! This would be the promised land that God had prepared for us in advance. So, in April 2012 we sold everything we owned and packed a few bags—plus a shipping container full of Henry's recording studio—and set out in faith toward what at the time seemed like nothing.

Once we finally arrived in America, I thought the time spent waiting for my dreams to come to pass had finally come to an end. I was like: *Okay God, we are here now. What is our assignment?* Well, even the Israelites had to fight the Canaanites who occupied the promised land, right?

Moving your family ten thousand miles across the world is enough to make you never want to move again. It had only been a little over four months since we left Australia, yet once again, I found myself knee-deep in boxes and packing tape. Two days before we were to leave our beautiful home in Melbourne, we received a phone call saying that the rental property we secured had fallen through. I couldn't believe it. All our belongings had left on a ship for America, and all we had left were a few suitcases and one-way tickets to the United States. I was so exhausted by this stage that all I could do was trust that the Lord was in control. I said, "If You called us to go, Lord, then You need to sort this out." And with that, I continued packing our bags.

We arrived on American soil on Easter weekend. We were temporarily homeless, so we checked into a hotel and prayed that God would soon find us a home. Our Realtor worked day and night to find a house that would be suitable for us and in our price range. This was no easy feat. One of our requirements was that the house needed a basement to fit Henry's recording studio. We couldn't believe how hard it was to find a basement or a room for a studio in Nashville. After all, it is Music City! After a long week of searching, we finally decided to rent a house without a studio. We would store Henry's equipment in the garage and then work out a better option later.

Discouragement began to set in. I had expected that when God said "Go," He would work out the details. I imagined that all we would have to do was move in and be ready to start our new life here in the United States. That was not the case. Sometimes things don't work out the way we plan, because God often has a better plan. Little did we know that what seemed like a setback was God's blessing in disguise.

If we had gone with the original rental property, it would not have been best for many reasons. Our Father is interested in the details, big and small. One of our greatest concerns in moving to the United States was our kids, who had left behind some very close friends in Australia. We had prayed with them that God would provide friends close by who they could connect with easily. Not only did God hear our prayers, He put us in a neighborhood that was filled with kids the same age. On top of that, we were able to rent the home on a short-term basis, which was unheard of amid the current market. That home turned out to be a blessing after all.

Within three months of settling into our new home, we were starting to get concerned that we still didn't have a place for the studio. The sound desk alone weighs a ton. We needed to find somewhere soon so that Henry could begin work. We were living off our life savings, and those funds were decreasing rapidly. Henry was unable to work with all his equipment stuck in storage, and I couldn't even secure a part-time retail position because I lacked experience. The feeling of discouragement returned, this time stronger than ever.

The waiting period can wear your faith down at times. One day, my faith was at an all-time low. It seemed as if God had forgotten us and we were stuck in a holding pattern, not able to go back and not able to move forward. Then I felt God lead me to listen to a particular podcast. As I began to listen, something shifted in my heart. I have found that the best thing to do when your faith is weak is go directly to the Word to build it up. Romans 10:17 says, "Faith comes from hearing the message, and the message is heard through the word about Christ." As I listened to the speaker, I sensed God's presence. I got down on my face before Him and cried out, "God, if this is Your will, then this needs to be Your bill!" I contended for the promise He had given us and did not get up until I felt a breakthrough.

The next day we had scheduled a lunch with a couple we met at church. We drove to their home and had a wonderful time getting to know them and listening to their story. They were also in transition and were moving to another country to plant a church. Their home had been on the market for some time, but it was not selling. They showed us around their magnificent home—and when we went downstairs, Henry and I both gasped. This basement was unlike any basement we had ever seen. It was amazing! We looked at each other and had the same thought: *This would be a perfect setup for a studio.* We left that afternoon and began to ask God for a place just like that.

Later that afternoon, Henry received a phone call. After he hung up, he said to me, "You are not going to believe what just happened!" The couple we had lunch with felt God tell them to take their house off the market and lease it to us. My jaw dropped. What a miracle!

Amazingly, this couple had been called to leave months before we had any idea we were being called to America. During that season, they also had times of discouragement and wondered what God was doing in their situation. A minister predicted they would do something with their home that was outside the box; he encouraged them not to worry and to trust God with the details. As we sat and ate with them, the Lord began to stir their hearts, saying this was what He had been planning! It was a win-win situation. We now had a studio for Henry to work in, and they had someone to care for their home as they moved on to their next season. This home would also be the birthplace of God's purpose for our lives. It was where our church, The Belonging Co., began. Right there in that basement was the beginning of our destiny.

The lesson I learned during this time is that God is always working on our behalf, even when we fail to see it. He has a perfect plan, and His timing is perfect. Our steps are always ordered by the Lord (Psalm 37:23). We cannot lean on our own understanding because it is limited (Proverbs 3:5).

The Lord opens doors that no one can shut and that no one else could open (Revelation 3:7). Don't despise the off-season. Keep investing in your call, your gift, your talent, your local church, and the people God has entrusted to your care. It is during this time that God is usually setting you up for what is to come.

Exquisite beauty, both internal and external, is the result of going through a process of preparation. No couture garment has ever been perfected without alterations. We need to see this process as the hand of God at work in our lives. The more we value each stage of the design process, even the ones of hardship, the more we will discover what we were tailor-made for.

Even powerful men of God had to go through a wilderness season:

- Joseph had a prophetic dream and a word from God, yet he spent seventeen years as a slave in prison before his dream was realized (Genesis 39:20–23).
- John the Baptist spent years in the desert preparing for a six-month ministry, only to be beheaded later (Matthew 3).
- Moses spent forty years in the palace and forty years as a shepherd before becoming the deliverer of God's chosen people (Acts 7:29–30).
- Paul was led into the desert of Arabia and Damascus for three years to learn from the Holy Spirit and to unlearn all his religious ways (Galatians 1:15–18). God wanted to readjust his thinking.
- Jesus spent forty days in the wilderness before His ministry began (Luke 4:1–2). He provided an example of what it means to follow the leading of the Holy Spirit into the wilderness, even if it means going from great community and recognition to solitude and temptation.

Those who prove to be faithful leaders respond in this manner when their time comes. This is what separates those who are called and those who are chosen. Submission to the

Lord's will is a necessary characteristic of a usable vessel of the Lord.

Deserts by their very nature are dry and desolate. They are also places of silence and seclusion. In biblical times, entrance into a wilderness meant that God was preparing the individual for new beginning. He leads us through times when physical and emotional resources are scarce. This is necessary to provide fertile ground for the seeds within us to grow. John 12:24 says: "Very truly I tell you, unless a kernel of wheat falls to the ground and dies, it remains only a single seed. But if it dies, it produces many seeds."

THE WILDERNESS SEASON

The movie *Reality Bites* with Winona Ryder and Ethan Hawke is one of my favorite films. In the movie, Troy, played by Ethan Hawke, says a line that has stuck with me. He is answering a telephone call and says, "Hello, you've reached the winter of our discontent." *The winter of our discontent.*[2] How many of us can relate to that season in our life?

When I think of winter, I think of everything being dead and barren. When you think of the wilderness, what do you imagine? Hardships, deserts, thirst, fatigue, danger, or loneliness? If you read the Old Testament, you will see that the Israelites roamed around in the wilderness for forty years before they entered the promised land. Because of this, I always viewed the wilderness as a negative place, one where you are trying to win God's favor back after being disobedient. However, I don't think the wilderness is always a bad thing.

The wilderness can be a terrible situation, or it can be a training ground that shapes you for the new season that lies ahead. It really is dependent on how you look at it. There are seasons when you must travel through a spiritual desert so God may nurture, shape, and prepare you for the work you have been called to do. Every great man and woman of God has gone through a winter of discontent. Their own wilderness, so to speak.

In the wilderness or desert experience, you cannot use the same tools or life skills that you use in your everyday life. For example, when you are at home with all your creature comforts, you can easily go to the fridge for food or take a shower with hot, running water. You have a bed to sleep in, and you can wash your clothes in the laundry. We take for granted how easy life is when the modern comforts surrounding us are readily accessible. However, if you were dropped off in the desert and left to fend for yourself, you would have to develop survival skills. There aren't refrigerators, beds, or showers, so you would be forced to think beyond your comfort zone and learn how to survive with what is around you. How are you going to feed and cover yourself in the wilderness?

This was my experience when I left Australia and came to America. I wasn't dropped off into a literal desert or wilderness, but I was in unfamiliar territory—outside of the comforts I had grown accustomed to. I had everything provided for in Australia: friends, a home, a car, a job, and a church. Then God called us to the United States. When I first arrived, it felt like a wilderness. My winter. A season whose cold bitter winds blew discontent. Nothing about this journey was familiar or easy. First, I had to navigate a new way of driving on the other side of the road. Second, I had to learn the road signs and their meanings.

Four months went by slower than a snail's pace, and I was mad. I was mad at myself, at my friends, at our temporary home, and at having gone to so many churches. The latter made me feel even worse because I could not find a church community to settle in. I felt alone and disoriented. I thought, *Surely, we have made a big mistake moving here.* I was certain God had abandoned me. I was not doing anything for the Lord. I wasn't working in a church, which is all I knew to do. I spent my days at home with my children, trying to find our fit in this new season of life. I found myself sleeping most of the day away, eating Kit Kats and sitting at the dining room table, staring at my computer and passing time looking at Pinterest. I had to force myself to go grocery shopping and cook dinner every night.

I didn't realize it at the time, but I was becoming depressed. I didn't understand that God was taking me to another level in living by faith. I had seen so many miracles leading up to our move to the United States that I assumed the red carpet would be rolled out for us upon arrival. I expected God would have a complete itinerary of what He wanted us to do.

In Australia, I had been serving someone else's vision. It was so easy to serve alongside someone who was making all the decisions and carrying the weight of every move the church made. I was a necessary tool in the toolbox used to build this amazing structure called the church. I didn't realize that season was required for me to find out what God's vision was for us in America. I was waiting for someone to hand me a recipe book on how to discover the will of God for my life so that I could just follow the directions. In reality, God was asking me to discover what the vision looked like and find Him in the process. I had to use the skills I'd developed in my past season to navigate this new season. My faith muscle needed to be exercised, as well as my trust muscle—and most importantly my *wait* muscle.

Here is a blog post I wrote during my wilderness season, in the middle of discovering my purpose in this new "winter"— when both ministry and vision seemed barren:

It's hard to believe that we have been in Nashville for ten months already. Driving on the other side of the road is beginning to feel natural, listening to American accents everywhere isn't abnormal anymore, and I have found that I have made the adjustment from the metric to imperial system easily. The pound has replaced the kilogram, Fahrenheit instead of Celsius, and kilometers are naturally being converted to miles. (Thank you, GPS!)

Overall, we have found a familiar rhythm that works for our family, and we are thriving. Even though things are beginning to feel familiar, I still feel like an alien at times. I looked up the definition of alien and it says: "A foreigner, especially one who is not a naturalized citizen of the country where they are living." That is true for me. I am a foreigner to the Americans that I meet on a daily basis. Even though I speak the same language, the American culture is a very different one from the Australian culture. I never thought I would be the odd one out, but it has helped me discover what I am really made of and who I really am. I get to determine from the beginning who I am when I meet new people. No longer is there a preconceived idea of who I am, who I'm married to, or what my background is. I am just Alex Seeley from Australia. The foreigner.

It has especially helped me in sharing my faith. I now get to tell everyone what I believe in my initial meeting with them. I have chosen to make my faith the most important fact about my life, not just the afterthought. It has been a refreshing change—one that I didn't even know would be such a gift from God. I have been given a new lease on life and a chance to do it differently. Have you ever asked yourself, If I had to do it over again, what would I change? Well, I got that chance. I am a resident alien; therefore, I am automatically labeled "different." So I decided to use the unique alien quality and make my difference more about Jesus and not just about being Australian. The effect has been staggering.

In just ten months, I have shared the love of Jesus every day with strangers and new friends. I have witnessed the power of the Holy Spirit at work in my everyday experiences. I have prayed for the sick, have had the privilege of leading people to Jesus, and have prayed for individuals to be baptized in the Holy Spirit. I have prayed for deliverance and counseled many who have experienced Christ's freedom. I have cried with people in coffee shops who have grieved the loss of loved ones and believed for miracles in play centers. I have invited many people over to my home and shared a meal, along with the love of Jesus. I have opened my home each week, and many people have gathered to worship and encounter His presence. I have given to the homeless and taken time to listen to strangers. This has all taken place outside of the church walls.

First Peter 2:11–12 says, "Dear friends, I urge you, as foreigners and exiles, to abstain from sinful desires, which wage war against your soul. Live such good lives among the pagans that, though they accuse you of doing wrong, they may see your good deeds and glorify God on the day he visits us."

As Christians, our lives need to stand out in a positive way from people in the world who do not know Christ. Our aim is not to be different for the sake of being different or to isolate ourselves from society; rather, our purpose is to live on purpose, to show that what we have living inside of us is the answer to what the world is craving.

I love being an alien in the city of Nashville, and I believe this is who we are meant to be on a daily basis wherever it is that we live, not just on a Sunday within the four walls of a safe church building.

During this season, I began to rediscover who I truly was without the title, without the paycheck, without the church position, and without the baggage. It was just me, and I found that inside my heart I was a daughter of God who loved people. I couldn't help but minister to others whenever I had the chance, and I received such joy in doing so. I realized that I loved to study the Bible even when I didn't have a sermon to write. I discovered intimacy with Jesus simply because I loved Him and had no other option. I had fallen in love all over again with the One I looked forward to connecting with daily. He became my first love again. That season was the most fruitful and beneficial season of my life, and I wouldn't change it for the world.

REDEFINING SUCCESS

Success does not mean you have arrived. In fact, in the middle of a season with favor and momentum, there is even more of a necessity to go further and spend time developing your gift and craft while no one is watching. If you become too comfortable, you may find yourself getting swallowed up by demands the world has placed on you. We were designed to do what we can and to allow God to do the rest. He gave us every gift, and He wants us to be good stewards of those gifts.

Success is not defined by the outcome, but by the process. We spend most of our lives imagining how great it will be when we become millionaires, teachers, wives, mothers, pastors, cover models, Grammy winners—and the list could go on and on. However, God sees our complete success during the process. Jesus wants us to become like Him, reflecting His image. He wants intimacy with us. That *is* the ultimate goal. It's a sobering thought, but it's also a relief from striving to become someone or something one day. Enjoy the ride, live for today, experience the joy of each moment, and be thankful in all things.

A NEW SEASON

Eventually, the season of wilderness came to an end. The days on the kingdom calendar turned toward a new season—one that was imperative for allowing the dryness of my heart to once again become soil for hope in finding Him.

Now that I'm a little older, I have gained a little more perspective. I now see the truth of those words spoken in that lecture during my first year of Bible college. Remember, my lecturer had said, "God always takes us through an apprenticeship season of about ten years before we walk the destiny He has for us." My apprenticeship lasted twenty years. The first ten years of my ministry life were a training ground of learning, serving, working my tail off, and doing things I never thought I expected. I set out chairs, drove teenagers to youth group, cleaned toilets, cleaned people's houses, photocopied copious amounts of paper, took meeting minutes, got coffees, shopped for others, ran errands, and so on. Through all those chores, God was preparing me for service. Another ten years were spent refining me and training me for a greater capacity. However, by gently nudging me to deal with the issue of unforgiveness, He was preparing me even more in the depths of my heart.

I am forever grateful for the process and am learning not to react when things do not go my way. Instead, I choose to yield to the process and allow God to do what He does best: bring about the purpose and vision He prepared in advance for me to do. Life will always have seasons, and we need to see the good in each of these seasons—for each season is necessary to bring forth much fruit in our lives.

Dear Lord,

Help me to yield to the process of the waiting periods of my life, knowing that You are preparing me to live out the plans and purpose You have for me. May I use these off-seasons to fall even more deeply in love with You and to learn Your Word and Your ways. I know You are good, and Your timing is perfect. Thank You for walking beside me during each stage of the design process, even the difficult ones, so I can discover what I have been tailor-made to do.

In Your name, amen.

CHAPTER FOURTEEN

FINDING YOUR
SENSE OF BELONGING

In order to be irreplaceable
one must always be different.
—Coco Chanel[1]

A s a young girl, I was full of dreams—desperate to escape
my boring life. I couldn't bear the idea that my future
might consist of getting up in the morning, going to work, coming home, watching TV, and going to bed—and then doing it all
over again until I died. Something inside of me knew there was
more to this life. I would daydream all the time and imagine
a wonderful life in which I was traveling the world, meeting
incredible people, and doing things that no one else had done.

One night, I was at the dinner table and declared my latest idea about what I thought I was going to be. My dreams changed weekly, sometimes daily. My mum, tired of me describing a new vocation every day, said, "By the time you make a decision to do something, you will be too old—and you will end up doing none of these things because you can't make up your mind and stick to one dream." I remember saying under my breath: "Well, I'll show you. Just you wait."

I love that about kids. One day they want to be a superhero, the next an astronaut, the next a scientist, the next a fashion designer—and the sky is the limit. They don't have any fear of failure. They believe they can do anything. Yet by the time they reach adulthood, many find themselves in jobs they hate because somehow their extraordinary dreams became ordinary. Maybe they followed their parents' lead or chose the responsible route. Or maybe at some point someone discouraged them, claimed it would be too hard for them, or said they should get their heads out of the clouds and come back to real life.

But what is real life? I believe we were all meant to be extraordinary. We are God's image bearers, created to be just like our Father. I love that humanity has achieved the impossible. We have made it possible to fly to the moon and live in space for a time. Extraordinary things like skyscrapers and sculptures and masterpieces are continually being created. God has designed each of us to be extraordinary and to live extraordinary lives.

An authentic life is beautiful. True beauty is visible when no façade exists to cover up our fears and fractures. Everyone loves the authentic over the counterfeit. And let's face it: we can all see through the fake. It's time to let go of the fear of others seeing our baggage—because we all have it. If we could just love one another instead of judging one another, then the world would look so much more beautiful.

THE COUNTERFEIT IS NEVER AS GOOD AS THE REAL THING

My first trip to Asia was an eye-opener for me. I couldn't believe how many market stalls were full of Chanel and Louis Vuitton and other high-end designer handbags—all bunched together on hanging hooks under a tent, or lying on the sidewalk in the middle of a busy street. Clearly, these were not authentic name-brand handbags, because you would never see bags displayed like that in a flagship store. A friend of mine purchased a Prada bag from Asia that looked beautiful from a distance, but within a few weeks, the Prada bag became a 'rada bag after the *P* somehow fell off. A few days later, the handle completely gave way and broke off while she was walking. I'm sure it was a fake considering it only cost her thirty dollars.

The differences between an authentic bag and a counterfeit include the quality of materials used, the time taken to produce the item, and the attention paid to detail. The label may look the same on the outside, but once you observe a counterfeit up close, you begin to see that the workmanship is of poor quality. It has been mass-produced by cheap machinery and with cheap materials. The heart of a master tailor has not been involved in the intricacies of design.

In the same way, if we choose to label ourselves a "Christian," our Christianity shouldn't just be a bumper sticker displayed on the back window of our car. Being a "Christian" is not about carrying the largest Bible or wearing the nicest suit to church. The label of "Christian" means that we are followers of Christ, so we should reflect the nature of Jesus that is living inside of us. Others should be talking about us in a positive way because of what they see coming from the inside pouring forth. We are displaying the brand of the kingdom of God. The quality of our life and actions should speak for itself and reveal Jesus to others. We don't need to declare our Christian identities. People should be able to see that we are Christians because we are like Christ.

There is something about fake that doesn't feel right. If someone were to buy me a counterfeit bag as a gift, I would feel ripped off. People will usually buy a counterfeit handbag for themselves because they say they cannot afford an authentic one, so they purchase a replica for a fraction of the cost. The original is always better than a copy, though. Its value is high for a reason.

Similarly, it is especially off-putting when people, not just things, are fake. There is nothing worse than trying to connect with someone but meeting only the façade and never the heart of that person. During my years of ministering in churches, I have come across this so many times that I started to wonder if anyone was authentic anymore.

The original is always better. It is comprised of valuable materials and intricate handiwork. The process is time-consuming and detailed, but the finished product is unique, original, and priceless. The counterfeit, on the other hand, is a copy. It was built with cheap materials, cheap workmanship, and cheap labor on a production line. The finished product is unexceptional, imperfect, unimaginative, and easily reproduced.

YOUR UNIQUE DESIGN

God's intention for the church, which is comprised of individual Christians, is to reveal the manifold wisdom of God that is to be made known to the world. Ephesians 3:10–12 tells us, "His intent was that now, through the church, the manifold wisdom of God should be made known to the rulers and authorities in the heavenly realms, according to his eternal purpose that he accomplished in Christ Jesus our Lord. In him and through faith in him we may approach God with freedom and confidence."

The word *manifold* means multidimensional or multifaceted, like a hologram that has many diverse colors and shapes no matter how you look at it. Therefore, each of us is created and purposed to reveal the multifaceted intelligence of God uniquely. If any one of us is not being original to who we are in Christ, and instead trying to copy someone else, then the world will never be able to experience that unique part of God that each one of us embodies. It's truly that important.[2] The Enemy distorts your view of yourself so you will black out that piece of the hologram, making God appear one-dimensional and boring. At times the church is guilty of producing clones, when churchgoers often look like the same dreary and boring representation of God. This is why many people today stereotype the church and are not able to see God's church for the unique beauty of diversity that it should be.

God didn't design us to be the same as any other person. That is why God, our Master Tailor, designed us with fingerprints that no one else on this entire planet has. As individuals, we cannot be compared to one another because we are one-of-a-kind masterpieces of priceless value.

Being original should never be difficult, since it is part of your DNA. It takes more effort to be someone else than it takes to be yourself. Don't ever feel the need to be like someone else. There is only one *you*. The fingerprints on your hands are original, and the pattern for your life is an original. Why copy someone else? Their life will never fit yours; therefore, you will constantly be adjusting your fit to feel right when it was never your size in the first place.

What sets us apart from every other person in the world? At the core of humanity is the desire to be original and celebrated for our uniqueness. No one wants to be a manufactured copy or a "one-size-fits-all" person. We all want to be remembered for something we did that made the world a better place. We want to be remembered as an individual. The more I focus on what others are doing, the less I focus on what makes me special and unique. The more I look at others and what they are achieving in life, the more I become profoundly fearful of my own capabilities. I start comparing my talents and abilities to theirs, which then causes me to wonder if I have fallen short on my end somehow.

I have come to understand that I cannot be someone else. I am me, no one else can be me, and I love who I am. The more time I spend focusing on my own strengths and gifts and using them to the best of my ability, the less I will feel inadequate. Through the lens of God's workmanship, I see myself as set apart and unique, which means I am irreplaceable.

I was once told that I was dispensable in the workplace. At the time, I remember feeling so hurt by that statement because I thought my boss was criticizing me. However, as I pondered on the thought a little longer, I realized the word cut deeper into my soul because it implied that *I* was replaceable. Yes, of course, someone else could be trained to do the work I was doing. However, what I brought to the organization could not be replaced. I brought more than just completing daily tasks; I brought life, joy, passion, and a unique ability to work with every colleague in that organization. No, I was not dispensable, because there wasn't another person who could work the way I did.

What inspires you? What makes you smile? What causes your heart to leap out of your chest every time you think about it? That is what makes you unique. Your dream or vision will not look the same as someone else's, and thank goodness for that! The last thing we need is a world full of copies of the same, boring thing.

Do what you love because you love doing it and make no apologies about it. God fashioned you for this. Take a risk. Step out in faith. God loves risk-takers because we need to totally depend on Him when we step out into the unknown. So many people die with all their potential locked up inside of them. God is not obligated to fulfill our potential. He designs us with everything we need to fulfill our destiny, but it is up to us to activate that potential and live it with passion and diligence.

Don't be afraid to fail. Failure occurs only when we give up, but trial and error is necessary to bring about something great. Unless we look within our own hearts and to God for inspiration, we will continually focus on what others have and what they are doing for inspiration. In doing so, we forfeit our unique God-given design that serves as a reflection of our Creator's magnificence. God is far from repetitive and boring, and He has a never-ending supply of new ideas and inspiration. Just look at creation across the globe, and you will see the beauty in so many diverse shapes, sizes, and colors. God never intended us to be ordinary; He designed us to stand out and be set apart to better reflect His glory.

Romans 8:19 says, "For all creation is waiting eagerly for that future day when God will reveal who his children really are" (NLT). The world is waiting to see the glory of God revealed through His children. But if we stay bound to our insecurities, then we will never step into the fullness of who we were created to be. Let us allow God's work in us to take place so that He can work through us and bring us to the place that He has already written about in His book (Psalm 139:16).

DISCOVERING WHERE I BELONGED

I used to resent where I came from and the cards that life dealt me. I always asked, "Why?" Comparison was my greatest enemy. I spent my days wishing for some else's life—wishing I looked different, wishing I had talents and gifts that others were celebrated for. I looked at what I didn't have rather than what I did have. I desperately wanted to feel I was accepted and that I belonged to something greater than myself, but instead I found myself feeling ordinary and unworthy.

It took many years before I understood that my life in God's hands was fashioned to a unique purpose. He would turn my mess into a message, my tests into a testimony, and my fractures and faults into fruit that others could taste and see that Lord has been good (Psalm 34:8). I learned that my life experiences, whether good or bad, seasons of plenty or seasons of lack, would set me on a course of discovering what I was made of and who I belonged to. God would point me to others like me, to help me bring breakthrough to the people that others would find it hard to relate to. My weaknesses in His power would become strengths, and every negative situation would be turned into a positive.

I began to see that the negative things that happened in my life, which were meant to destroy me, actually became the part of me that can help other people find freedom. No longer did I search for a new family to belong to; I was grateful for mine. Even though my family was far from perfect, I began to see the good in how I was brought up. My dad gave me a strong work ethic, and my mum gave me a love for English literature. My mum always dressed us in impeccable clothing, which developed my love of fashion and design. My dad taught me how to manage my finances and be independent in my career.

Looking back, now I see the strengths that I have developed over the years. Since I was a child, my deepest longing was to be able to help people. Perhaps it's because I longed to be helped so much. I came alive when talking to people and helping them through their own struggles. I felt I could help save people from despair. Little did I know that God had placed in my heart purpose for a life of ministry to others. Because of my experiences, I can empathize with people who have gone through similar situations and give them the keys to finding their freedom. Suddenly, my life makes sense and I understand my purpose. God turned around what the Enemy meant for evil, and He made it beautiful.

The moment I stopped striving to be someone else because I thought I didn't measure up—that's when I began to see my true beauty. When I let go and accepted every fracture and frailty, my life went from ugly to beautiful. Being vulnerable and transparent didn't bring more shame; instead, my honesty enabled others to feel safe and break free. They could say, "If she can do it, then so can I." My life began to inspire others, and that caused me to thrive.

I truly believe we are meant to inspire others to freedom and to help them discover who they are in Christ. We should imitate the characteristics of Jesus in others, not imitate their individuality. God gives us grace to enable us to live according to His plan and purposes. And this grace has been tailor-made just for you, because God knows how much and what type of grace you need to succeed.

Because we have been made in God's image, He designed our purpose to be about others. In Philippians 2:5–11, we learn that when Jesus walked the earth as a man and lived for thirty-three years in human form, He made himself of no reputation. He was obedient to the Father until death on a cross. He came to serve humanity, not to be served by us. Because of this process, God gave Him the name above every name, and the Bible says that all creation will bow down to Him one day and say that He is "King of kings and Lord of lords!" Yes, He is the Son of God, but His purpose was, and is, about us. John 3:16 says, "For God so loved the world that he gave his one and only Son, that whoever believes in him shall not perish but have eternal life." God's plan has always been for us to collaborate with Him, to help bring the kingdom of God to this earth and bring order to a world of chaos.

God designed each of us to be unique, yet we must be seamlessly connected and unified to serve together and have maximum impact in this world. However, unity does not mean uniformity. God gave us special gifts for a reason, and we should celebrate our diversity and not fear others looking or being different from us. As Christians, we are one body with many parts. Sadly, there are some of us who despise our part.

Sometimes we want to be the head because the head is at the top, but the toe is just as important. A chair fell on my big toe once, and I was certain I had broken it. It was one of the most painful experiences I'd ever been through. It disabled me from doing anything. I couldn't think straight until the pain had lifted and the toe had healed. I understood just how needed my big toe was when it was injured. We are all called to be parts of a body that work together, and when all the parts are in unity, we can expect the best results.

God created us for a unique purpose that enables Him to establish the bigger picture. If we can only realize how important our part is, then we will no longer strive to fulfill a part that is not ours.

The secret to finding our true identity is not a magic potion or a diet plan or a quick-fix pill. It is simply a life surrendered to Jesus—when we discover that our sense of belonging comes from Him and Him alone. Everything else flows out of that love relationship. When we yield our lives to Him and take one step in the right direction, then we will look back and see the changes that have taken place. Our true identity lies in the consistency of showing up, turning up, saying yes, dying to self, serving others, loving unconditionally, and forgiving those who hurt us. Day by day you may not notice the change, but after a while, you will look back and see how far you have grown. You will finally see things through the filter of the person you were tailor-made to be.

> *Dear Lord,*
>
> *I surrender my life fully to You, knowing that You have tailor-made me for Your unique purpose. Help me to understand the role that only I can fulfill and to stop striving to fulfill a part that is not mine. Today, I will take the first step in the right direction in order to find my sense of belonging in You.*
>
> *In Your name, amen.*

THE AUTHENTIC YOU

The authentic self is soul made visible.
—Sarah Ban Breathnach[1]

W e are the most at ease when no one is watching. We are free to be ourselves and act the way we feel at the moment when no one is there to judge us.

When I took my daughter, Holly, to her first concert when she was six years old, we had to wait in the lobby before the doors opened to the arena. There were hundreds of people standing around waiting to take their seats. Music was playing through the speakers, and her favorite song came on. Holly began dancing like no one else was in the room, even though all eyes were on her. She did not care what any other person in that room thought. I sat there mesmerized by her freedom, and I sensed the Lord saying to me at that moment, *This is how I designed every single one of My sons and daughters to be—secure enough to be completely at ease with themselves.*

Holly is still like that to this day. She has a confidence that is attractive, and she is secure in who she is because she feels loved and affirmed by her earthly parents and her heavenly Father. We should all take a leaf out of her book.

FROM MESS TO MASTERPIECE

For years, a tug-of-war took place in my heart and mind. I nearly gave in to Satan's lies, believing I was insignificant and worthless. But one day I met Jesus, and I allowed Him to come into those broken spaces and hold my hand through the process and show me what it truly meant when He said, "I have come that they may have life, and have it to the full" (John 10:10). When I handed over control to Him and gave Him my life, I did as He asked.

Jesus was so kind to walk me patiently down this road. He began shedding the hurt and hardened layers of my heart ever so gently, so as to not overwhelm me. And as I drew close to Him, He drew close to me (James 4:8). I discovered a friend who truly is closer than a brother (Proverbs 18:24), and He has never left me or forsaken me (Hebrews 13:5). His purpose is for me to know Him intimately, and through that relationship, to discover who I am. And I did! I discovered that I am a daughter of the King of kings. I have been fearfully and wonderfully made (Psalm 139:14). I was predestined before the foundation of the world to do good works, which He had prepared in advance for me to do (Ephesians 2:10). He transformed my brokenness so that the world can see how He truly gives beauty for ashes (Isaiah 61:3). He turned my sorrow into joy (Jeremiah 31:13), and He took me out of slavery and made me an heir with Him (Galatians 4:7).

He gave me the keys that helped me forgive and restore my relationship with my mother. Now I couldn't love her more. She has become a pillar of strength to me, and she is my greatest cheerleader.

Understanding my tailor-made design has helped me become a better wife, mother, and friend, and my life is truly abundant beyond measure. Is it perfect? No! But it sure is a masterpiece. If I had continued listening to Satan's "one-size-fits-all" lies, I likely would have failed at marriage, been filled with anger, taken it out on my children, and continued struggling with my eating disorder—which I could have passed down to my daughter. But because of the grace of Jesus and the alterations He made as I yielded my life to Him, I continue to marvel at how beautiful my life truly is. Were it not for Jesus, I would never have been able to write this book, because He tailored every chapter and altered every paragraph to make it a couture, one-of-a-kind masterpiece.

Our lives are waiting to be revealed on life's catwalk. The world needs to see the magnificent design He has been making in you. God intends your life to inspire others when they look at how magnificently you have been designed. You reflect the unrivaled work of your Master Tailor. The labels you now choose to wear should reflect the Designer who created you.

The first word ever spoken over me at birth was the word *special*. It was God's truth over my life. The world tried to convince me otherwise, and I spent my childhood and young adulthood trying to rediscover the first label I ever received. *Special* is a word I used to resent, because I felt anything but special. Years later, as I look at the definition of *special*, I see that it has several meanings—including "better, greater, or otherwise different from what is usual; exceptionally good or pleasant; belonging specifically to a particular person or place; designed or organized for a particular person, purpose, or occasion."[2] This is exactly who we are to God. We are special. We are one-of-a-kind, and we have been designed to belong to Him. He has created us with an extraordinary purpose. When we understand that this is the core of who we are, we can then live from a secure place. We can truly discover the secret to who God designed us to be.

MY PRAYER FOR YOU

I pray that this book has helped you understand that no matter what your past looks like, you are God's masterpiece—and He is waiting to reveal His design to you. He wants you to give Him your whole heart. Allow the Pioneer and Perfecter of your faith to bring about what was always intended for you (Hebrews 12:2).

Sure, some trimming will be involved as the Master Tailor cuts away the fabric that is not needed. Sure, the process will take time; the Master Tailor needs time to work on His creation, time to pause and reflect for inspiration, or time to do no work and rest. Sure, testing and change will be unavoidable, as the Master Tailor demands repeated alterations to find the perfectly fitted garment hidden between stitches and excess fabric. But the process is the beautiful journey wherein the Master Tailor's vision is fulfilled and the garment displays His design. The unique process was designed just for you.

A ONE-OF-A-KIND CREATION

It was my senior year formal, and I was so excited to dress up and celebrate. All the girls talked about for months prior to the event was what they would wear. Everyone was elated about shopping for the perfect dress. I, on the other hand, was about to do something I had never done before. I was having a dress exclusively designed and tailor-made especially for me. My aunty was a professional seamstress who made exquisite clothing for the women in our town who loved high-end, one-off pieces that were hand sewn to perfection. I couldn't wait to be measured for my aunty to design my very own dress that no one else would have.

The finished product was breathtaking. It was a perfect black lace dress—off the shoulder, with silk buttons all the way down the back. It fit me like a glove. I stood in front of the mirror at the final fitting and felt so special. This dress had been designed specifically for me and made to my exact measurements. It was mine, and I felt like a million dollars.

You are a priceless, one-of-a-kind creation, and you have permission to shine the glory of God on earth as it is in heaven. God's plans for you are good, and you were made for a purpose that only you can fulfill. So get out there and be who God created you to be before the foundations of the world—and make no apology for it!

Remember this: You are special! You have been tailor-made for a purpose more beautiful than any masterpiece that has ever been designed. And you belong to the Master Tailor, our Lord Jesus Christ.

IT'S YOUR TURN

It's time to make this content real in your own life. As you've been reading, I've been praying that you would clearly hear God's voice speaking to you, telling you that you are indeed special. A one-of-a-kind creation.

I'd like to ask you to sit for a moment and close your eyes. Remove any distractions. Wait to hear God's voice. Allow Him to direct you to verses in your Bible that speak His truth into your life. This process will help you replace any lies that may have been spoken over you with His truth.

As God speaks to your heart, write down the beautiful things He says to you. When you're finished, go back through this book and read over the prayers at the end of each chapter to open any other thoughts He may have for you.

No matter what your past looks like, remember that you are God's masterpiece. You've been tailor-made!

_____

_____

IT'S YOUR TURN

IT'S YOUR TURN

_____

_____

_____

_____

_____

_____

_____

_____

_____

_____

_____

_____

_____

_____

_____

_____

_____

_____

_____

_____

_____

_____

IT'S YOUR TURN

ACKNOWLEDGMENTS

B efore I believed I could write, God strategically placed people in my life to help this dream become a reality. I was fearful to put pen to paper, but I knew I needed to do this project. There are a few people to thank, as this book took many years to come to fruition.

First, I would like to thank my husband, Henry, for that night back at Summit Crescent when you looked at me and said sternly, "Stop talking about writing a book and just write it!" That was the push I needed to stop procrastinating and begin telling my story.

Fast-forward a few years to my friends and family in Nashville—my promised land. Little did I know that God was preparing an army of people to be fellow soldiers in this great fight of faith. Thank you, Mia Dunnavant, who sat with me in my kitchen and began to rearrange the words that I had first written down many years ago. In a few short sentences, you helped make the introduction of my life sound so good. You gave me the confidence to keep writing.

A huge thank you goes to Stephanie Hughes, who came into my life at a time when I desperately needed help putting together my cacophony of words and making sense of a manuscript that was a whole lot of words poured out.

To Cameron Shadinger, who came to my home with her toddler on a weekly basis for a short season to help shape words with me and encouraged me every time we met that this story needs to be told. I will be forever grateful for that time spent with you. To Shelly Griffin: If not for you I would not have had a manuscript to present to my agent at all. Your genius and your eloquence are breathtaking. You fueled me to the end and helped me bring it to the finish line.

Thank you to Lisa Harper, my dear friend who believed in me and championed me to pursue writing. She is a brilliant and seasoned author herself, yet she took the time to set me up to win and followed through with her promise. Thank you for the introduction to Lisa Jackson, to whom I will be forever grateful. The first time we spoke on the phone I knew in my spirit she was a kindred heart. I felt like I had known her for decades. Thank you for understanding my heart and for being the best agent there is.

Thank you to Debbie Wickwire and the W Publishing team, who didn't just want to meet me when deciding whether to publish me but came to see the core of my heart: The Belonging Co. It's when you came to see what God was doing in our midst that I knew that you were my publisher. Thank you for making this process so much fun and for your attention to detail. Your heart toward God's message being delivered is beautiful, and I will always be grateful you gave me the opportunity to write my first book. I would also like to thank Sam O'Neal for his amazing editing skills and for his kindness. He always went the extra mile and has helped bring this dream into reality.

Thank you to James Goll, Jason Ingram, Jonas Myrin, and Mary Tran for reading my manuscript and giving me the best feedback. It was an honor for me to have your brilliance and discernment critiquing my work. Thank you to my Belonging Co. family, who have also been one of the greatest gifts that God has ever given me. I could never have dreamed to have such a supportive church who loves the presence of God as much as I do. I'm so thankful to the entire community of our church that makes me want to get up every morning and serve you and lead you well.

Last but certainly not least, thank you to my family back in Australia. To Mum, Dad (who is in heaven), Toni, Bruno, and David. I love you all more than you will ever know and am so grateful that you are my family. Without each of you, I would not be the person that I am today. I wrote this for us.

NOTES

Introduction: What Label Are You Wearing?
1. *Random House Kernerman Webster's College Dictionary*, s.v. "tailor-made."
2. *Collins English Dictionary*, 12th ed., s.v. "tailor-made."

Chapter 1: Design or Accident?
1. C. S. Lewis, *The Weight of Glory* (New York: HarperOne, 2001), 46.

Chapter 2: The Original Design and How It Became Flawed
1. Lisa Bevere, CHERISH Conference Keynote (lecture, C3 Church, San Diego, CA, October 20, 2012).
2. Patty LaRoche, "The Ultimate Fixer Makes the Impossible Possible," *Fort Scott Tribune*, July 30, 2010, www.fstribune.com/story/1653152.html.

Chapter 5: How Jesus Changes Everything
1. *Oxford Living Dictionaries*, s.v. "splendor."

Chapter 6: Insecurity Is Not a Good Look on Anyone

1. Julie Ma, "Diane Von Furstenberg on Warhol, the Wrap Dress, and Men in Turtlenecks," *The Cut*, January 14, 2014, www .thecut.com/2014/01/dvf-at-lacma-on-warhol-the-wrap-dress -more.html.
2. *Merriam-Webster*, s.v. "insecurity."
3. Louie Giglio, *How Great Is Our God* (Atlanta, GA: Six Step Records, 2009), DVD.

Chapter 7: Who Is My Father?

1. P. D. Eastman, *Are You My Mother?* (New York: Random House, 1960).
2. *Collins English Dictionary*, 12th ed., s.v. "spitting image."

Chapter 8: Forgiveness Unlocks Freedom

1. Amy Rees Anderson, "'Resentment Is Like Taking Poison and Waiting for the Other Person to Die,'" *Forbes.com*, April 7, 2015, www.forbes.com/sites/amyanderson/2015/04/07 /resentment-is-like-taking-poison-and-waiting-for-the-other -person-to-die/#1896b01f446c.
2. Jack Zavada, "Justification: What Is Justification in Christianity?" *ThoughtCo.*, April 13, 2016, www.thoughtco.com /what-is-justification-in-christianity-700688.
3. *Baker's Evangelical Dictionary of Biblical Theology*, s.v. "sanctification," www.biblestudytools.com/dictionaries /bakers-evangelical-dictionary/sanctification.html.

Chapter 9: The Process Is the Destination

1. Don Eisehauer, "Helping Us Face the Inevitable End of Life Issues," *DocPlayer*, January 2017, docplayer.net/34457059-H -e-l-p-i-n-g-u-s-f-a-c-e-t-h-e-i-n-e-v-i-t-a-b-l-e-e-n-d-o-f-l-i-f -e-i-s-s-u-e-s-by-dr-don-eisenhauer-acc.html.

Chapter 10: History Repeats Itself

1. *Oxford Living Dictionaries*, s.v. "renounce."

Chapter 11: The Make or Break of Circumstances

1. Charles Swindoll, *David: A Man of Passion and Destiny* (Nashville: Thomas Nelson, 2000), 72.

Chapter 13: From Desert to Destiny

1. Tony Robbins's Facebook page, April 5, 2015, www.facebook.com/TonyRobbins.
2. This quote is originally from Shakespeare, *Richard III.*

Chapter 14: Finding Your Sense of Belonging

1. Marcel Haedrich, *Coco Chanel; Her Life, Her Secrets* (New York: Little, Brown, 1972), 255.
2. I am indebted to Pastor Eric Johnson from Bethel Church in Redding, California, for the ideas behind this content.

The Authentic You

1. Nikki Martinez, "25 Quotes in the Importance of Being Your Authentic Self," *Huffington Post*, December 12, 2016, www.huffingtonpost.com/dr-nikki-martinez-psyd-lcpc/25-quotes-in-the-importan_b_13744706.html.
2. *Collins English Dictionary, 12th ed.*, s.v. "special."

ABOUT THE AUTHOR

Alex Seeley, born and raised in Australia, spent seventeen years on the pastoral team at a worship movement in Melbourne where she and her husband, Henry, helped pioneer a church that grew to more than ten thousand people. After relocating to Nashville in April 2012, they began opening their home on Tuesday nights for people to worship, encounter God, and build genuine community in a city where many live life "on the road." In a few months, The Belonging Co. was born and has quickly become known as a place to find freedom. Each week they now reach more than three thousand people across Nashville, and thousands online from all over the world.

Not only are Alex and Henry coleaders and senior pastors of The Belonging Co., they are also proud parents of two children, Holly and Taylor."

```
THE
BELONGING
CO
```

After relocating to Nashville, TN, in April 2012, Henry and Alex Seeley began opening their home on Tuesday nights for people to worship, encounter God, and build genuine community in a city where people's personal and spiritual lives often succumb to the transient nature of "life on the road."

During their first meeting with just a handful of people, something profound happened—the presence of God filled the room and every person there had an encounter with God in a fresh and tangible way. Continuing to meet every other week, it only took a few months before their basement was at capacity and The Belonging Co. was born.

After two years of meeting together, The Belonging Co. now reaches over 3,000 people across Nashville and thousands online from all over the world. We can't put into words what God is doing, but we are sure about one thing: He is building His church and changing people's lives from the inside out.

We desire encounter over entertainment, intimacy over industry, presence over presentation, people over position— and most of all JESUS over everything.

WWW.THEBELONGING.CO